If the
TABLE
Could
TALK

A TASTE of the
HOLIDAYS

If the TABLE Could TALK

A TASTE of the HOLIDAYS

Alyssa A. Alia

Recipes and Food Styling by Alyssa A. Alia
Photographs by Al Owens

MALANGA PUBLISHING

If the Table Could Talk...what would it say?

*Alyssa Alia, a prominent New York area food stylist and mother of two,
shares her most cherished Holiday recipes from her table to yours.*

*Captured by the menus she's saved from decades of Holiday celebrations,
you'll find within these pages a treasure trove of well-loved family recipes -
delectable, fun, easy-to-prepare and filled with joy! These recipes, developed
and prepared lovingly by Alyssa over many years, are presented here with
time-saving tips, make-ahead tricks, decorating ideas and hints for
how to make every gathering you host a success.*

*Beautiful photography brings each recipe in this cookbook to life,
a testament to Alyssa's talent as a food stylist.*

*So, sit back and enjoy Alyssa's menus, her food journal through time,
and let it inspire you to create your own food memories with family and friends!*

Prop Styling and Photo Art Direction by
Michele Jerry of Limoncello Productions

Book Design and Art Direction by
Nancy Hourihan of Red Relish Creative
Lisa Curran of Creative Designory

Managing Editor: Marisa Malanga
Assistant Copy Editors: Maria Malanga, Donna Saiewitz
and Jack Hourihan

Food Styling Assistants: Maria Malanga, Marisa Malanga,
Christopher McMahon, Geovanna Colindres, Donna Saiewitz
and Tracy McKenna

Published and Produced by Malanga Publishing/
Triple A Productions, LLC

ISBN 978-0-9981313-4-4

First Edition

 www.alyssaalia.com

 @Alyssa Alia Food Stylist

 @alyssaalia

 alyssa alia food stylist

 Alyssa Alia

 Alyssa Alia

"For my incredible Mom & Dad, who taught me to do what you love and have a passion for, and you will excel beyond your dreams. I love you with all my heart."

Alyssa xo

Contents

A Taste of the Holidays

Foreword

When one visits Alyssa as her guest, by merely entering her home, you feel like you are in a hallowed temple dedicated to love and hospitality, all built around ingenious foods and her will to teach the countless joys of food. Her book projects this passion she has to spread her knowledge and her love, inducing all in her aegis to the good life based on her extraordinary feelings of hospitality.

I have been privileged to be a part of Alyssa's family for many, many years, starting with a wonderful friendship with her father, Anthony, with whom I attended high school. Through his lifetime, I observed him raising his charming family with discipline, strong morals and most notably, compassion and love for people. I believe it was this strong upbringing that has fostered Alyssa's tenacious personality and commitment to the highest standards for every aspect of her life, including her drive to entertain and to teach people the highest standards of food preparation and hospitality.

Alyssa doesn't just prepare a meal, she creates an unforgettable experience, and you can taste the love and enthusiasm in every last morsel. My fondest memories have been of sitting around the Sunday dinner table with Alyssa, Tom and their lovely daughters sharing stories, laughter and a fabulous meal.

Alyssa is a totally genuine person and her generosity nourishes the soul as well as the body. Now you, too, can experience her creativity, ingenuity and culinary brilliance while forging your own cherished memories around your table with family and friends by following her lessons she so lovingly brings to the arena to enrich lives. Alyssa is a most rare human soul who exudes unquenchable enthusiasm, charm and entertainment skills for all to enjoy.

Arthur E. Imperatore, Sr.

A Letter from Alyssa

Happy Holidays from my table to yours. "If the Table Could Talk - A Taste of the Holidays" is the sequel to my first solo cookbook "If the Table Could Talk - A Taste of Celebrations." When my team and I started shooting, we intended to do one cookbook, but I loved the photos so much that I wanted to feature them exclusively by separating the menus into two cookbooks rather than one. In this way, you can make more food memories with your family and friends with these specific holiday menus filled with beauty, yumminess and joy! That's what my food is all about. If you create a wonderful meal, it then creates an experience where people come together around your table and share not only your food, but also the simple act of love. I believe the holidays are the best ways to bring loved ones around your table. My goal is to give you recipes that will become your holiday favorites that will last a lifetime and for generations to come. My daughters make my holiday recipes from Halloween to the classic seven fish Italian Christmas Eve to Easter Sunday, and every dish is filled with memories because they grew up with me making these for our family and friends. By passing them on, not only do the food memories live on, but also the legacy we leave for our children, family and friends through the taste, smell, look and feel of these homemade and home-loved dishes.

If your table could talk, what would it tell you? The holidays bring back my most heartfelt and treasured memories because of the food associated with it around my family's table. Whether it be an everyday dinner with your children or a celebratory occasion, every moment that you gather and share food at the table brings people together. I wanted to recreate these memories by sharing recipes that were served around my table with love throughout my life. I have said, so often, that eating and enjoying meals around the table reinforces the most precious and special memories of family and friends. The menus in this book are a lifelong autobiography, a recorded memoir of my cherished holidays, milestone events and impromptu occasions at my table. My first menu on record was celebrating my engagement to my husband. I invited my future in-laws over my parents' house and hand wrote my menu in calligraphy. I still have that menu over 30 years later. That first menu inspired me, from then on, to write menus for every event I cooked in my home. I have hundreds of them. They are a treasured journal through time. I am so thankful to reminisce and savor every recipe that was shared at my table with loved ones, because it brings back the best memories. Whether it was celebrating Halloween in costumes with friends or Thanksgiving with its hearty, fall comfort food, or the seven-fish Christmas Eve with over 40 family members because Italians treasure this holiday and tend to have a ton of cousins, the memories will live on through these prized and tantalizing recipes.

I have been a lover of food and passionate about cooking since I was three years old. I have been a professional food stylist for over 30 years, so I have included delicious photographs with every recipe throughout the book that I prepared and food styled for your enjoyment.

My goal is to fill your cravings and desires through these irresistible photographs. I truly believe a picture captures 1,000 mouthwatering memories and it is my hope that these photographs entice you to try them all—to anticipate every bite. I invite you to enjoy this sampling of recipes from my menus that hold a special place in my heart. They are easy and fun, and most are even make-ahead. Many were inspired through family and holiday traditions, and others from friends, professional and personal. I have also included shopping and entertaining tips with time saving ideas and helpful tricks. Since my professional life is styling food in the most beautiful way it can be for the camera, I have also included easy garnish and serving suggestions to make your parties showstoppers with minimal fuss and ease.

But make me one promise before you begin—make these recipes your own, especially when serving your loved ones. These selected and special holiday recipes are so close to my heart, so share them so you can begin new, heartfelt traditions or update your recipe collection. There are no limits to the culinary arts. The beauty of sharing recipes is to make your own new creations. Redesign them for your needs and tastes, and create a whole new food experience. Please use these recipes simply as guides to make new memories around your table.

Thank you for this special opportunity to share my life-filled love of food alongside you.

Sending you warm wishes, love, culinary bliss and blessings for all your holiday seasons.

Keep your table talking!

En-JOY and cook just for the love it,

Alyssa xo

About The Author

I can still remember standing next to my grandmother, my Nana, with my chin-counter height, cutting the struffoli for Christmas at age four! I enjoyed every kitchen moment and became an essential assistant for all of my family's meals. Food prep became a culinary obsession and my family encouraged me to pursue my talents in the kitchen. My favorite Christmas gift was my first electric mixer at ten years old, a stainless Sunbeam Mixmaster. I was obsessed with this mixer and polished it every time I used it. I still have it to this day.

Growing up in an Italian household exposed me to cooking traditions, family Sunday dinners and healthy food preparation on a daily basis.

At 12 years old, I started baking with my neighbor, Mrs. Betty Ann Maryott, who could have been a successful pastry chef herself. Every cookie she made was picture perfect! She lovingly taught me after school, at her house, my first official cake decorating lessons. I began to cake decorate everything I could, starting my art skills and patience for perfect results with practice, practice, practice. Our next door neighbor, Mrs. Kovak, was an excellent Czechoslovakian baker. She taught me the meaning of technique and the importance of patience in pastry making. I couldn't wait to help and watch her make her homemade strudel pastry dough on Saturday afternoons.

At 16 years old, my Mom saw a help wanted sign in the window of a small gourmet store front called Cooktique in Tenafly, New Jersey, near where we lived in Closter. I applied and was hired as the owner's runner and assistant for two summers and on weekends during the school year. The owner, Silvia Lehrer, gave me my first opportunity to work in a professional culinary atmosphere and I was hooked the minute I walked into her store. She also had a small cooking school in the back of the store where she taught classic cooking classes. I was the shopper, prepper and food gopher while demonstrating the newest craze, the Cuisinart Food Processor! Here is where I learned one of my most valuable cooking lessons, especially to make stock, stock and more stock. She would also have guest chefs for a few weeks each summer to teach specialty classes and promote their first cookbooks. I was able to assist the renown French chef Jacques Pépin and the famous Italian chef noted for his extraordinary pasta making, Giuliano Bugialli. What a thrill and I didn't even know what celebrities they would become! I was just enamored by them - I was in cooking heaven. This was my passion and that is when I knew I wanted to pursue a career in food.

I also worked as a Friendly's waitress the last three years of high school. Here is where I learned my people skills as well as service skills. I believe every person should be a waiter or waitress at least once in their lifetime. It makes you appreciate all kinds of people and teaches you how to accommodate while making them feel happy, even if it's for a moment. People will appreciate your kindness and pass it on.

During that time in high school my dad encouraged me to write to the food editors of national magazines to ask them how to pursue a career in the culinary arts. This was life-changing advice as many of them wrote back with college choices and even class suggestions. I was accepted to Cornell University and obtained a bachelors degree in nutritional sciences but I still was longing for more culinary training.

For two college summers, my Dad also thought I should apply as an intern at the Lipton Company, now known as Unilever, where I was asked to work in the food science department. They introduced me to the Lipton Test Kitchens down the hall. This department developed and tested recipes for their food products and, again, I realized I needed to be in a kitchen environment. After graduating from Cornell, I was hired as a Test Kitchen Home Economist at Lipton and worked there for three years. I learned so much about the corporate food industry but I still longed for more advanced culinary training. I decided to leave Lipton and enrolled into a full time culinary chef program at the New York Restaurant School in New York City. I fell into my heaven and loved the training every day in my chef whites. I graduated with a chef certification with honors. Soon after, the school sponsored students for some extra training at Le Cordon Bleu, France, my dream school!

After returning from Europe, I applied to many food magazines in New York City. One of the food editors, Jean Voltz, remembered my high school letter and hired me several times as a freelancer. I continued to freelance, over three years, for numerous publications. It was here where I performed more recipe development but then I would also be asked to go into the photography studio to food style the recipes for the camera. Everything started to click together for me. My food science training at Cornell, my culinary passion, love of food art, and then my professional culinary training - it was the perfect blend to become a professional food stylist. I continue to freelance as a food stylist presently. I have food styled over the years for many major food companies as well as magazines, for print, packaging, film, advertising, social media and video applications. It has been a whirlwind career path but I have loved every minute of it. This profession trained me to create on the spot, keep my cooking skills sharp, prepare efficiently and therefore perform quickly and effortlessly with patience and kindness at every job. Food styling is almost like performing on stage, it's live and you are as good as your last job. There is no room for mistakes so practice and preparation are key. Your food is your musical art while your client is your audience and ultimate critic. You want the best reviews every time.

All my years of experience and polished culinary skills helped me to be efficient in my home kitchen for entertaining as well as feed my family in a moment's notice. As a working mother of two, I had a demanding career but I used honed skills to my advantage in every cooking event that crossed my kitchen.

This book is a tribute to my life learning that made me not only the professional I am today in my craft but the excited home cook who just loves to be in the kitchen, everyday, just for the love of it!

New Year's Eve

New Year's Eve

Nana's Eggnog

Limoncello

Limoncello Champagne Cocktail

Festive Deviled Eggs

Honey Drizzled Ricotta Bruschetta *with*
Raspberries and Manchego

Spicy Shrimp Skewers *with* Prosciutto and Pea Pods

Smoked Salmon Wraps *with* Creamy Herbed French Cheese

Fabulous Fresh Pesto

Parmesan Prosciutto Wraps *with*
Pesto and Roasted Red Peppers

Filet Mignon Bruschetta *with*
Caramelized Pears and Gorgonzola

Watercress, Endive and Shaved Fennel Salad *with*
Manchego and Apricots

Lobster Roll Sliders

Caramel Candy Cheesecake Bars *with* Pecans

Helping my Nana
make her famous Eggnog
is one of my most vivid holiday
memories. It uses raw eggs, so it's very
important that the eggs are either pasteurized
and/or very fresh. The work is well
worth it! It has a kick which explains
why everyone was so happy on
New Year's Eve.

Nana's Eggnog

8 egg yolks
¾ cup confectioner's sugar

Beat in large saucepan until well combined.

½ cup rum
½ cup brandy
1 cup whiskey
1 quart whole milk
Pinch of salt

Add to saucepan. Cook, whisking constantly, on low heat until slightly thickened, about 10 minutes or until reaches 160°F with instant-read thermometer. (NOTE: Do not overcook or mixture will become scrambled eggs.) Chill, 30 minutes.

8 eggs whites, room temperature

In bowl of electric mixer with whisk attachment, beat until soft peaks form.

¼ cup confectioner's sugar

Slowly add sugar to egg whites and beat on high speed until stiff peaks form.

2 cups (1 pint) heavy cream

In a second bowl of electric mixer with whisk attachment, beat heavy cream until soft peaks form. Fold into egg white mixture.

½ cup confectioners' sugar
2 teaspoons vanilla extract

Continue beating and slowly add confectioners' sugar. Add vanilla extract.

Fold heavy cream mixture into chilled custard mixture.

Sprinkle, if desired, with ground nutmeg Serve immediately. Sprinkle, if desired with ground nutmeg.

TIPS:

Cooked egg mixture can be made one day ahead. Refrigerate with plastic wrap placed directly on egg mixture to prevent a skin from forming.

Custard mixture can be whipped just before serving.

To prevent any chance of Salmonella contamination, please use pasteurized eggs.

Makes about 12 Cups Eggnog, about 24 Servings

Limoncello

2 (750 milliliter) bottles 90 proof good quality grain alcohol

1 (1.75 liter) or 2 (750 milliliter) bottle 80 proof good quality vodka

45 large lemons (scrubbed and washed)

Pour all alcohol in large gallon-type glass jars (Found in kitchen supply stores or sun tea jars work great, too.)

Using a potato/vegetable peeler or paring knife, carefully peel off just the yellow skin of lemons. It's very important the white part under the peel (also known as white pith) is removed underneath the lemon peels, or else this will make mixture bitter. Make peels as large as possible to make it easier later when straining. Place peels in alcohol.

Cover tightly and store in cool (not cold) dark place so alcohol can extract oils from peels to create an infusion.

Makes about 5 to 6 Quarts

This depends on evaporation and how long you marinate mixture.

Allow to sit for at least three weeks to three months. Stir gently every few days. The longer the lemon peels sit, the better the color and flavor. A good test is to take one lemon peel and see if it snaps when you bend it. If it does, it's ready.

6 cups bottled or distilled water

8 cups sugar

Bring to a boil in large saucepan over medium high heat and simmer, about 5 to 10 minutes or until sugar is completely dissolved. Let cool completely.

Strain lemon mixture into another large gallon-type glass container using a large, fine mesh strainer and large coffee filters. (This takes time and is a little messy.) Repeat straining process.

TIPS:

It's terrific as a cordial served with my Citrus Biscotti (see page 206) after dinner and delicious over vanilla ice cream.

Start saving glass bottles from any home decorating store early, making sure that the tops are airtight. The corks can also be waxed closed, if desired, to make sure they are well-sealed.

Add cooled syrup to strained alcohol and see limoncello come to life as it turns a bright yellow color. At this point, pour limoncello into pretty glass bottles with cork tops.

Return to cool, dry place for at least another two weeks.
After two weeks, keep in freezer for three to six months.

Limoncello is an Italian liqueur made from lemons. It originated from Italy's Amalfi Coast (Capri, Sorrento and Liguria) from their famous giant lemons. It's served ice cold from the freezer as an aperitif or after dinner.

This recipe has created many treasured lifelong friendships at our home celebrations, restaurant and other numerous occasions. I make a double batch (a case of lemons usually has around 90 lemons) and start my batches in the summer. It also makes a perfect, elegant gift that will definitely impress, especially during the holidays.

Limoncello Champagne Cocktail

1 cup Limoncello (See page 18)

1 (750 milliliter) bottle
Champagne or Prosecco

} *Pour and divide evenly into
8 champagne flutes*

2 lemons, thinly sliced } *Garnish and serve*

*Makes about
8 Servings*

*Use the Limoncello
(See page 18) you have carefully
made to make these spectacularly
bubbly cocktails to ring in the
New Year!*

Festive Deviled Eggs

1 dozen large eggs

*Makes 24
Deviled Eggs*

In large saucepan, cover eggs with cold water and bring to just a boil (not a rolling boil or eggs yolks will oxidize and edges will turn green instead of bright yellow). Immediately remove from heat. Cover and let sit, 15 minutes. Immediately drain and rinse with cold water.

Crack eggs and peel under cold water, peeling from bottom end first. Pat dry. Cut eggs in half lengthwise and remove yolks into medium bowl. Mash with fork. Place whites on serving platter.

¼ cup mayonnaise

2 tablespoons sour cream
or plain Greek yogurt

½ tablespoon Dijon mustard or
1 teaspoon dry mustard

1 tablespoon fresh lemon juice

Salt and white pepper

*Combine until smooth.
Fill egg whites evenly with yolk mixture using pastry bag fitted with star tip or with teaspoon. Garnish with suggested toppers.*

Festive Decoration Toppers:

Red and black caviar with chives

Smoked salmon with capers and dill

Sprinkle of smoked paprika

Sprinkle of chipotle chili pepper,
Manchego shavings and chopped scallions

Drizzle, if desired, with truffle oil
for extra special flavor

TIPS:

Take small slice off bottom of white before filling so they don't roll over on platter.

Did you know that older eggs peel more easily than fresher ones? Egg yolk shrinks away from its outer membrane near shell, making a little air pocket. Use eggs that have been in refrigerator for about one week when hard cooking them. Peeling hard cooked shells will now be easy and effortless.

Easy poppers for guests to grab as soon as they arrive. My daughter Marisa loves decorating these. Try her festive topping suggestions.

These appetizers make such a gorgeous presentation and are a scrumptious combination of flavors. The sweetness of the ricotta and honey complements the saltiness of the Manchego cheese.

Honey Drizzled Ricotta Brushetta
with Raspberries and Manchego

1 long baguette,
thinly sliced diagonally (about ¼-inch)

2 tablespoons extra virgin olive oil

Brush bread slices and grill or broil until toasted.

1 container (15 ounces)
whole milk ricotta cheese

Top each bread slice with rounded tablespoon.

1 pint raspberries

4 ounces Manchego (or Parmesan cheese),
shaved or very thinly sliced

Garnish on top of ricotta.

¼ cup honey

Drizzle.

Makes about 24 Servings

TIP:

Can make toast one hour ahead of time before your quests arrive.

Flavorful and spicy!

Spicy Grilled Shrimp Skewers *with* Prosciutto and Pea Pods

1 pound large shrimp, cleaned, with tails on

1 cup pea pods

12 thinly sliced prosciutto (about 4 ounces)

> *Wrap shrimp with prosciutto and pea pod. Skewer with long toothpick.*

½ cup pepper sauce

½ teaspoon ground ginger

> *Mix together. Brush on skewers. Place on foil-lined lightly greased baking sheet.*

Broil, 5 to 8 minutes, or until shrimp are pink and done.

Makes sbout 8 Skewers

TIP:

Can be assembled one day ahead and broiled right before serving.

Smoked Salmon Wraps *with* Creamy Herbed French Cheese

1 package (6.5 ounces) creamy herbed
French cheese (little more than ½ cup)

1 lemon, zested

2 tablespoon fresh dill, snipped

Mix together in small bowl until smooth

6 (8-inch) spinach tortillas or
any flavor of your choice

*Divide. Spread cheese mixture evenly,
about 2 tablespoons per tortilla.*

12 ounces smoked salmon, about 18 slices

*Divide evenly and top on cheese mixture in
single layer, about 3 salmon slices on each
tortilla. Roll up tortillas. Tightly wrap in
plastic wrap. Refrigerate at least 2 hours.
To serve, slice wraps on an angle into 1-inch
slices.*

*Makes about
24 Pieces*

TIPS:

*Alternate with Parmesan Prosciutto Wraps
(see page 33) for an elegant appetizer tray.*

*Garnish with lemon wedges and
extra dill sprigs.*

Fabulous Fresh Pesto

2 cloves garlic

1 large bunch Italian parsley,
stems removed (about 1 cup)

1 large bunch fresh basil leaves,
stems removed (about 2 cups)*

Add to food processor and process until smooth.

½ cup extra virgin olive oil

¼ cup pignoli nuts**

¼ grated Parmesan cheese

¼ cup grated Pecorino Romano cheese

Squeeze of a lemon (about 1 tablespoon)

Salt and pepper

With food processor running, slowly drizzle in olive oil. Add pignoli nuts, cheese and salt and pepper.

Makes about 1½ Cups Pesto

TIPS:

*If you want to keep pesto extra green try blanching the basil. To blanch basil, dip basil leaves in boiling water, 2 to 5 seconds. Immediately plunge in ice water bath. Remove and pat dry.

**Can substitute with walnuts or almonds.

*Toss on your favorite pasta.
Also great on fish and poultry.*

Freezes beautifully up to three to six months! Make small containers or fill ice cube trays to have small amounts handy for everyday cooking, too.

We grow tons of basil in our garden in the summer. It's my ultimate herb!

My favorite flavor combination is basil and garlic. My husband and I love our garden in the summer. He is in charge of the tomatoes and vegetables, while I am in charge of the herbs. I plant extra basil for pesto all summer long. Then we freeze big batches to enjoy during the holidays.

Another delicious appetizer wrap. The prosciutto combined with the pesto creates the savoriest, boldest Italian flavors.

Parmesan Prosciutto Wraps *with* Pesto and Roasted Peppers

6 tablespoons prepared pesto (See page 30)

1 lemon, zested

} *Mix together in small bowl until smooth.*

6 (8-inch) whole wheat tortillas or any flavor of your choice

} *Divide. Spread pesto mixture evenly on tortillas, about 1 tablespoon per tortilla.*

12 thin slices prosciutto (about 3 to 4 ounces)

12 thin slices provolone (about 3 to 4 ounces)

} *Divide evenly. Top pesto in single layer, about 2 slices each.*

1 jar (12 ounces) roasted red peppers, drained, patted dry and sliced into thin strips

3 cups baby arugula (about 5 ounces) or your favorite lettuce

2 tablespoons Parmesan cheese, shaved

} *Layer on top of prosciutto and provolone. Roll up tortillas. Tightly wrap in plastic wrap. Refrigerate at least 2 hours. To serve, slice wraps on an angle into 1-inch slices.*

Makes about 24 Pieces

TIPS:

Alternate with Smoked Salmon Wraps (see page 28) for an elegant appetizer tray.

Garnish with lemon wedges and fresh basil leaves.

Filet Mignon Bruschetta *with*
Caramelized Pears and Gorgonzola

1 loaf Italian bread or baguette, thinly sliced diagonally (about ⅛-inch each to make about 24 slices)

2 tablespoons fig jam

Spread on slices.
Bake, 2 to 3 minutes, or until melted.

2 tablespoons extra virgin olive oil

1 beef tenderloin (about 2 pounds), trimmed and tied

Salt and pepper

Salt and pepper tenderloin. Heat large heavy ovenproof skillet on medium heat. Add olive oil and seasoned tenderloin. Brown on all sides, about 5 to 8 minutes.

½ cup red wine (your favorite)

Add to tenderloin in skillet and allow to evaporate. Place tenderloin on roasting pan. Roast, 10 minutes or until 145°F for medium rare, or a few more minutes for medium. (NOTE: Use an instant-read thermometer to prevent overcooking.) Let rest, 10 minutes.

2 tablespoons butter

4 small pears

½ lemon, juiced

Meanwhile heat butter in large heavy skillet. Cook pears on medium heat until browned, about 5 minutes. Squeeze on lemon.

½ lemon, juiced

1 tablespoon honey

Combine and drizzle onto pears. Set aside.

2 cups baby arugula or watercress

4 ounces gorgonzola, crumbled

To assemble:
Slice tenderloin into ¼-inch slices. Top bread with sliced tenderloin, watercress, prepared pear topping and gorgonzola.

TIPS:

Ask bakery to slice your Italian loaf or baguette to save time.

Beef tenderloin can be made one day ahead.

Warm in low 300°F oven 10 minutes before slicing.

Makes about 24 Pieces

The combination of sweet pear, gorgonzola and filet of beef will make your mouth sing!

Watercress, Endive and Shaved Fennel Salad
with Manchego and Apricots

Dressing:

¾ cup extra virgin olive oil

¼ cup Champagne vinegar
or white wine vinegar*

1 tablespoon Dijon Mustard

¼ cup Italian parsley, chopped

Salt and pepper

Combine and set aside.

Salad:

1 bunch watercress
or baby arugula (about 5 ounces)

2 Belgian endives, thinly sliced
(green or red)

1 bulb fennel, thinly sliced

1 small head radicchio, thinly sliced

1 cup dried apricots, halved

½ cup pomegranate seeds

1 cup Sugar & Spice Glazed Holiday Pecans
(see page 171)

Assemble in larger serving bowl or shallow platter. Toss, right before serving, with dressing mixture.

TIP:

*Substitute Champagne vinegar or white wine vinegar with your favorite wine vinegar.

*Makes about
8-10 Servings*

It's a contrasting concoction of bitter greens and sweetness with a touch of licorice. The Champagne vinegar adds more sparkle to the holiday.

These special lobster sliders can be made ahead so you can enjoy your evening while making quite an impression on your guests.

Lobster Roll Sliders

¼ cup mayonnaise

2 tablespoons sour cream
or plain Greek yogurt

1 tablespoon Dijon mustard

1 lemon, zested and juiced

1 teaspoon dry crab seasoning

2 dashes hot pepper or Sriracha® sauce

2 green onions, chopped

1 red bell pepper, finely chopped

Salt and pepper

Combine in large bowl.

1 pound cooked lobster meat,
torn into large pieces

*Add to mayonnaise mixture and toss well.
Chill.*

24 potato slider rolls

¼ cup butter, melted

*Slice tops vertically. Brush with
butter. Toast lightly. Stuff center with
lobster mixture.*

*Makes 24
Appetizers*

TIPS:

*Brush melted butter inside slider rolls and
toast on grill pan for a buttery crisp crust
before serving.*

*Lay lettuce down on toasted slider rolls for
extra crunch and a beautiful presentation.*

A perfect combination of cheesecake, caramel, pecans and a chocolate cookie crust.

Caramel Candy Cheesecake Bars *with* Pecans

Preheat oven to 350°F.

*Line 9 x 13-inch baking pan with heavy-duty aluminum foil, extended
over edges of pan. Spray with non-stick cooking spray, line with parchment paper
and spray again. (Remember BPB: The butter, paper, butter rule in baking.)
This prevents bars from sticking to bottom of pan and create easy removal. Set aside.*

Crust:

*Makes 24
Bars*

1 package (14.3 ounce) chocolate sandwich
cookies (36 cookies), finely crushed in
food processor

½ cup (1 stick) butter, melted

2 tablespoons sugar

1 tablespoon instant espresso

*Combine in bowl. Press firmly into prepared
pan. Bake 8 minutes. Cool.*

Reduce oven to 325°F.

Batter:

3 (8 ounces each) packages
cream cheese, softened

¾ cup sugar

*Combine in large bowl of electric mixer.
Beat on high speed, until light and fluffy,
about 5 minutes.*

3 large eggs

*Add one at a time and beat on low speed
until blended, about 1 minute. DO NOT
OVERBEAT. (This also helps prevent
cheesecake from cracking.)*

1 tablespoon all-purpose flour

½ teaspoon salt

1 teaspoon vanilla extract

*Add and beat on low speed until smooth,
about 1 minute. Pour mixture over crust
into prepared baking pan.*

*Bake 30 minutes or until center is almost
set and edges are golden. Let cool on wire
rack. Chill, at least 2 hours.*

*Lift cheesecake with foil on long sides to
remove carefully. Cut into bars, straight
down with one motion, with long slicing knife
that has been dipped in hot water and dried.
This will help make a perfect clean cut.*

1 package (8 ounces) caramels,
melted according to package directions

24 pecan halves

*Place 1 tablespoon of caramel onto each bar.
Top with pecan halves.*

2 ounces semi-sweet chocolate, melted

TIP:

Bars freeze beautifully up to two weeks.

*Place in small disposable plastic sandwich
bag or piping bag. Cut small opening at
bottom corner of bag with scissors. Drizzle
chocolate over bars. Refrigerate until serving.*

41

Easter

Easter

Antipasti Selection
Red and Golden Beets with Feta and Fresh Mint
Fava Beans with Sun-Dried Tomatoes and Parsley
Farro with Roasted Peppers, Eggplant and Olives

Fresh Marinara

Homemade Manicotti Crepes *with* Fresh Marinara

Grilled Lamb chops *with* Rosemary

Maple Glazed Spiral Ham *with* Pineapple Salsa

Three Cheese Old-Fashioned Scalloped Potatoes

Balsamic Glazed Asparagus Wrapped *with* Prosciutto

Pizza Rustica

Lemon Scented Ricotta Tart *with* Shortbread Crust

Lemon Bars

Dark Chocolate Dipped Coconut Macaroons

Biscotti Sicilian-Style *with* Dark Chocolate and Cherries

Red and Golden Beets *with* Feta and Fresh Mint

Preheat oven to 400°F.

4 medium red beets, tops removed
4 medium golden beets, tops removed

Place each color separately on large piece of aluminum foil.

2 tablespoons extra virgin olive oil
Salt and pepper

Coat beets with olive oil. Season with salt and pepper. Wrap foil around beets. Bake, 45 to 60 minutes or until tender when poked with fork. Let cool. Rub skin off with paper towel. Cut into 1/4-inch chunks. Place in medium bowl.

¼ cup extra virgin olive oil
2 tablespoons raspberry vinegar
1 tablespoon Dijon mustard
2 cloves garlic, chopped
Salt and pepper

Combine with beets. Chill for at least 2 hours.

½ cup feta or ricotta salata, crumbled
2 tablespoon fresh mint, chopped

Add and toss before serving.

Makes about 4 Cups

TIPS:

Beet mixture can be made one day ahead. Keep beet colors separate so the red does not bleed into yellow, then combine when serving.

Garnish with fresh mint leaves.

Beets were my Mom's favorite, so this recipe is in memory of her.

Fava Beans *with* Sun-Dried Tomatoes and Parsley

4 cups dried fava or lima beans*,
soaked for 4 hours or overnight

2 teaspoons salt

> Bring to a boil in medium saucepan.
> Cook, 10 minutes or until tender. Drain.
> Add to medium bowl.

1 lemon, zested and juiced
1 cup sliced sun-dried tomatoes in oil,
drained, and use 1 tablespoon of oil
½ cup Italian parsley, chopped
¼ cup extra virgin olive oil
2 tablespoons red wine vinegar
Salt and pepper

> Combine with beans.
> Chill for at least 1 hour.

TIPS:

Best served at room temperature.

*Can substitute with canned beans.

Makes about
4½ Cups

Fava Beans
(otherwise known as broad beans)
are like big lima beans, but slightly
sweeter. I had these for the first
time in Italy and just loved them!
They are considered good luck in
Sicily since they were a big factor
in saving Sicilians during a time of
famine. The fresh ones are
hard to come by so here is
my version with dried.

Farro *with* Roasted Peppers, Eggplant and Olives

Makes about 7 Cups

Preheat oven to 400°F.

1 medium eggplant }

Place on baking sheet. Bake, 45 minutes or until tender with fork. Let cool slightly. Peel skin and cut into 1/4-inch chunks. Place in medium bowl.

2 cups farro
4 cups chicken stock* or water
1 teaspoon salt }

Bring to a boil in medium saucepan and reduce to low heat, covered, 20 minutes or until tender. Drain any excess liquid. Add to eggplant.

1 jar (12 ounces) roasted red peppers, drained
1 can (6 ounces) medium black olives, drained and quartered lengthwise
½ cup Italian parsley, chopped
3 garlic cloves, chopped
½ cup extra virgin olive oil
¼ cup red wine vinegar }

*Add to eggplant mixture**. Chill, at least 1 hour.*

12 basil leaves, sliced chiffonade (stack and roll basil leaves, then slice into strips) }

Add and cook for 30 minutes until bubbly.

Salt and pepper }

Add right before serving.

TIPS:

*(See page 94), for Chicken Stock recipe or use your favorite boxed chicken broth.

**Eggplant mixture can be made one day ahead.

Choose whole grain farro because it has a slight chewiness like barley, which combined with these Mediterranean ingredients, makes a wonderful addition to your antipasti spread.

Fresh Marinara

8 cloves garlic, chopped
¼ cup extra virgin olive oil
} *Cook on low heat in large skillet, 5 minutes or until soft but not browned.*

2 cans (28 ounces each) San Marzano plum tomatoes, undrained
} *Add. Blend with an immersion blender right in the skillet until smooth (or puree in blender before adding to skillet).*

10 basil leaves, sliced chiffonade (stack and roll basil leaves, then slice into strips)
Salt and pepper
} *Add. Cook for 30 minutes or until bubbly.*

Makes about 8 Cups

TIP:

Recipe can be easily halved but I suggest making this big batch and freezing it in small containers. Can be frozen up to three to six months.

The secret to the ideal marinara - a sweeter and stronger tomato with less seeds. My parents always used San Marzano tomatoes growing up as classic, Italian traditions play a major role in my cooking.

Homemade Manicotti Crepes *with* Fresh Marinara

1 cup water

1 cup eggs (about 4 to 5 large eggs)

1 cup all-purpose flour

1 teaspoon salt

Combine in blender and whirl until smooth. Pour into large measuring cup. Let sit, 10 minutes.

1 container (15 ounces) whole milk ricotta cheese

8 ounces (about 2 cups) shredded mozzarella cheese

½ cup grated Parmesan cheese

2 eggs

¼ cup Italian parsley, chopped

Salt and pepper

Combine thoroughly in large bowl. Chill until ready to use.

Heat non-stick medium skillet (8 inches) or crepe pan over medium heat. Spray with non-stick cooking spray. Ladle or pour ¼ cup batter, swirling to cover bottom. Crepes set very quickly. Turn crepe over as soon as edges start to curl up a little with fingers or rubber spatula. Heat only a few seconds. Place on parchment-lined cookie sheet.
Repeat with parchment paper in between each crepe to prevent sticking.

Scoop ricotta filling with ¼ cup measuring cup and place down center of crepe. Fold ends over filling and place seam side down in greased shallow baking dish.

2 cups fresh marinara (see page 48) (or your favorite red sauce)

Spoon marinara evenly over prepared manicotti.

2 tablespoons shredded or grated Parmesan cheese

Sprinkle over marinara.

Preheat oven to 400°F.

Bake, 25 to 30 minutes or until heated through.

TIPS:

Garnish with fresh basil leaves.

Add 1 cup fresh or frozen chopped spinach, squeezed dry, to filling for extra touch.

Manicotti can be made and assembled one day ahead.

Makes about 12 Manicotti

All of our holiday dinners include a pasta course. This was one of my Mom's favorite recipes. I learned to make it at a very young age and it's a great recipe to do with a partner.

Grilled Lamb Chops *with* Rosemary

6 cloves garlic, chopped

6 sprigs fresh rosemary, leaves
removed and slightly chopped

6 sprigs fresh thyme, leaves removed

Salt and pepper

¼ cup extra virgin olive oil

} *Combine.*

8 (1½-inch thick) loin or rib lamb chops*

} *Marinate with herb mixture in refrigerator,
1 hour.*

Preheat oven to 400°F.

1 tablespoon extra virgin olive oil
¼ cup white wine (your favorite!)

} *Heat grill pan or heavy skillet
(enamel or cast-iron that is ovenproof)
on medium high heat. Add oil and then
marinated lamb chops. Cook until browned,
about 2 to 3 minutes per side.*

*Add wine. Place skillet in oven and cook,
6 to 8 or until an instant-read thermometer
reaches 120°F for rare, 125°F for medium
rare and 130°F for medium.*

*Allow to rest at least 2 to 3 minutes before
serving.*

*Makes about
4 Servings*

TIPS:

**If you are using rib lamb chops, decrease
time by 3 minutes in oven and watch
carefully. Do not overcook.*

Recipe is easily doubled or tripled.

*Garnish with additional fresh rosemary
sprigs.*

Lamb is the traditional entrée for an Easter celebration. Lamb chops are easy to prepare and also make a beautiful centerpiece selection for any special occasion.

This makes a gorgeous center piece for any buffet table!

Maple Glazed Spiral Ham *with* Pineapple Salsa

Ham:

Preheat oven to 300°F.

1 spiral sliced ham (8 to 10 pounds), bone-in

1 cup pineapple juice

Place in roasting pan. Add pineapple juice to bottom of pan. Cover and bake, 1½ hours or until tender. Increase oven temperature to 400°F.

1 cup maple syrup

½ cup brown sugar

½ cup pineapple juice

2 tablespoons Dijon mustard

1 teaspoon cinnamon

1 teaspoon nutmeg

½ teaspoon cloves

½ teaspoon ginger

Combine in medium saucepan. Bring to a boil. Brush on ham and bake, uncovered, 30 to 40 minutes or until browned and edges look glazed and crisp.

Pineapple Salsa:

1 pineapple, coarsely chopped (about 3 cups)*

1 red pepper, chopped

1 small red onion, chopped

2 scallions, chopped

1 clove garlic, chopped

2 tablespoons maple syrup

One lime, zested and juiced

½ bunch cilantro**, chopped

Combine in bowl and serve with ham.

Makes about 12 Servings

TIPS:

* Can substitute with canned pineapple chunks, drained.

** Can substitute with Italian parsley if not a cilantro lover.

Garnish with fresh cilantro leaves and lime slices.

Pineapple Salsa can be made one day ahead.

Three Cheese Old-Fashioned Scalloped Potatoes

Preheat oven to 375°F.

Lightly grease a shallow 2-quart casserole dish or 9 x 13-inch baking dish.

¼ cup (½ stick) butter

4 cloves garlic, chopped

1 large shallot, chopped

Heat butter in large skillet on medium heat until melted. Add remaining ingredients. Cook until fragrant and translucent, about 2 to 3 minutes.

¼ cup all-purpose flour

Stir in with wire whisk. Cook on medium heat, 2 minutes.

1½ cups whole milk

1 cup heavy cream

Salt and pepper

Whisk in and bring to a boil. Cook on medium heat until thickened, stirring constantly, about 5 minutes.

½ cup grated Parmesan cheese

¼ cup grated Romano cheese

1 cup (4 ounces) grated Fontina cheese (Gruyere or Gouda can be substituted)

Stir in until melted.

3 pounds Yukon Gold or new potatoes, thinly sliced (I prefer to keep skins on, but you can peel them if you'd like.)

Alternately layer half of potatoes and sauce in prepared casserole dish ending with cheese sauce.

1 tablespoon grated Parmesan cheese

1 tablespoon grated Pecorino Romano cheese

Sprinkle on top. Bake, 40 minutes or until tender.

Let stand 20 minutes before serving. (This will allow potato mixture to settle and it's easier to cut.)

TIPS:

Keep sliced potatoes in ice water while preparing sauce to prevent them from turning gray.

Entire recipe can be made ahead and assembled one day before baking and serving.

Garnish, if desired, with fresh thyme or chopped parsley.

Makes about 12 Servings

I just love this version of a great make-ahead comfort food. I added an Italian twist to this traditional dish.

The asparagus
is nuzzled deliciously with
the subtle saltiness of the
prosciutto and the sweetnees
of the balsamic glaze.

Balsamic Glazed Asparagus Wrapped *with* Prosciutto

1 tablespoon extra virgin olive oil

Heat grill or grill pan and brush with oil.

1 bunch thin asparagus
(about 1 pound, 30 spears)

*Wash and trim about 1-inch off ends
on a slant.*

16 thin slices prosciutto
(about 6 to 8 ounces), cut in half lengthwise

*Wrap asparagus with prosciutto slices.
Place on baking sheet.*

1 lemon, juiced
1 tablespoon balsamic glaze
Salt and pepper

*Combine and brush onto asparagus.
Broil, 3 to 5 minutes or until tender
but still "al dente."*

*Makes about
10-12 Servings*

TIPS:

*Can be made four hours ahead.
Serve at room temperature.*

Pizza Rustica

2 pounds whole milk ricotta cheese

5 eggs

2 cups (8 ounces) mozzarella cheese, shredded

¼ cup grated Parmesan cheese

4 ounces thinly sliced prosciutto, chopped

¼ teaspoon ground nutmeg

Preheat oven to 350°F.

Combine well in large bowl.

2 pounds Italian sausage, casings removed

Cook in large skillet over medium heat until nicely browned, stirring and breaking it up occasionally, about 5 to 10 minutes.

3 cloves garlic, chopped

Add to sausage drippings. Cook, 2 minutes or until fragrant. Drain excess drippings. Add to cheese mixture.

Italian Pastry Dough* (or use store-bought refrigerated pastry dough)

Press two-thirds of dough lightly to fit bottom and sides of 9-inch springform pan. Piece together if dough breaks apart.

Makes about 16 Servings

Fill springform pan with cheese mixture. Roll out remaining one-third of dough on floured surface to 12-inch circle. Place dough over filling. Pinch crusts together and crimp edges for decorative finish. Make a few slits on top to allow steam to escape.

1 egg yolk mixed with 1 teaspoon water

Brush crust with egg wash.

2 tablespoons grated Parmesan cheese

Sprinkle on top.

Similar to a deep dish quiche but firmer, it's a combination of cured Italian meats, cheeses and eggs covered with pastry dough. It's inspired by my Grandma Alia who I never met but who wrote a recipe column in the 1930's.

Bake, 50 to 60 minutes on bottom oven rack until crust is golden brown. Cover top of crust with aluminum foil if gets brown too quickly.

Let cool 10 minutes on wire rack and unlatch springform pan so it doesn't stick. Let cool completely before serving.

TIP:

Pizza Rustica can be made up to three days ahead and stored in refrigerator.

*Italian Pastry Dough:

3 ½ cups all-purpose flour
¾ cup (1½ sticks) cold unsalted butter, cut into pieces
¼ cup cold solid vegetable shortening, cut into pieces
1 teaspoon salt

Process in food processor until mixture resembles small peas.

3 large eggs

Add one at a time, pulsing after each addition to combine.

2 to 4 tablespoons ice water

Add 1 tablespoon at a time and pulse until dough JUST forms a ball. (DO NOT OVER PROCESS. This will cause the butter to melt and make dough tough.)

TIP:

Dough can be made one week ahead and kept in refrigerator or freeze up to one month.

Divide dough into 2 pieces, (about two-thirds of dough in 1 piece and one-third in the other). Wrap in plastic wrap and chill, about 30 minutes, to rest dough.

I saw this handwritten
on a small piece of paper in my
Grandmother Alia's favorite recipe envelope.
It took me a while to test and make it
perfect the way I think she would have
wanted it to be.

Lemon Scented Ricotta Tart *with* Shortbread Crust

Preheat oven to 350°F.

Open springform pan. Insert the bottom pan upside down and close springform pan.
Line 9-inch springform pan with circle of parchment paper.
This method allows the tart to slide right off onto your serving plate much easier.

Wrap outside of springform with heavy-duty aluminum foil to prevent
any seeping of butter through pan when baking.

Crust:

1¾ cups all-purpose flour

⅓ cup sugar

teaspoon salt

1½ cups (3 sticks) butter, cut into cubes

2 egg yolks

1 small lemon, zested

Combine in food processor pulsing until comes together into a ball. Press into bottom of prepared springform pan. Bake 10 to 12 minutes or until lightly golden.

Batter:

2¼ cups whole milk ricotta

½ cup sugar

2 eggs, lightly beaten

½ cup heavy cream

1 teaspoon vanilla extract

1 small lemon, zested

½ teaspoon salt

Combine in large bowl of electric mixer. Beat on medium high speed until well blended, about 2 minutes.

Pour batter into prepared pan.

Place on middle rack of oven. Bake 45 minutes or until middle is almost set. Let cool. Chill 2 hours or overnight.

Makes about 12 Servings

TIPS:

Serve, if desired, with pitted black cherries and syrup or your favorite fruit topping.

Dust with confectioner's sugar for extra specialness.

Can be baked and frozen up to one month ahead.

Lemon Bars

Preheat oven to 350°F.

*Line 9 x 13-inch baking pan with heavy-duty aluminum foil, extended
over edges of pan. Spray with non-stick cooking spray, line with parchment paper
and spray again. (Remember BPB: The butter, paper, butter rule in baking.)
This prevents bars from sticking to bottom of pan and create easy removal. Set aside.*

Crust:

3½ cups all-purpose flour
1½ cups confectioners' sugar
1½ cups (3 sticks) butter, melted

} Combine in medium bowl.

*Press into bottom of prepared pan.
Bake, 15 minutes or until slightly golden.
Let cool slightly, about 5 minutes.*

Filling:

3 cups sugar
½ cup all-purpose flour
2 teaspoons baking powder
½ teaspoon salt

} *Combine in large bowl.*

6 eggs, slightly beaten
3 lemons, zested
½ cup lemon juice (about 5 lemons)

} *Add to dry ingredients. Mix with wire whisk
until smooth.*

*Pour over crust.
Bake, 25 to 30 minutes or until topping
is slightly golden and slightly firm to the
touch.*

TIPS:

*Remove from pan holding ends of
aluminum foil.*

*Removing entire lemon bar from pan makes
cutting easier. Use long slicing knife that
has been heated under hot water and dried,
cut straight down in one swoop to avoid
tearing the lemon bars. This will allow for
the perfect clean cut, every time.*

Let cool. Chill for at least 2 hours.

*Lift lemon bars with foil on long sides to
remove carefully. Cut into bars or triangles
straight down, with long slicing knife that
has been dipped in hot water and dried.*

*Dust with additional confectioner's sugar
before serving.*

*Makes about
32 Bars*

Through trial, error and
the love of lemon bars, this recipe
was created. The buttery shortbread crust
perfectly contrasts and compliments the
lemony curd topping. This recipe is
dedicated to my Big Sis,
a true lemon lover!

Dark Chocolate Dipped Coconut Macaroons

Preheat oven to 325°F.

Line baking sheets with parchment paper.

1 package (14 ounces) flaked coconut

1 can (14 ounces) sweetened condensed milk

1 teaspoon vanilla extract

1 teaspoon coconut extract (optional)

½ cup sliced almonds, toasted

½ teaspoon salt

Combine in large bowl. Set aside.

2 large egg whites

In large bowl of electric mixer, beat until soft peaks form. Fold into coconut mixture. Drop heaping tablespoon of batter on parchment-lined cookie sheet, about 2-inches apart.

Bake, 12 to 15 minutes or until slightly golden. Let completely cool on wire rack.

8 ounces dark or semi-sweet chocolate, coarsely chopped and melted

Dip cooled macaroon bottom in chocolate. Place on prepared baking sheets. Let harden at room temperature or chill to set faster.

Makes about 30 Macaroons

TIP:

Sprinkle with coarse sea salt before serving for sweet and salty decadence!

Chocolate coconut cream eggs were, and still are, a favorite found in Easter baskets at our house. I created a cookie version and dipped them in chocolate to make an Easter-worthy treat.

Biscotti Sicilian-Style *with* Dark Chocolate and Cherries

Preheat oven to 350°F.

Line baking sheets with parchment paper.

½ cup unsalted butter (1 stick), softened

2¾ cups sugar

} *Add to large bowl of electric mixer. Beat on high speed until light and fluffy, about 5 minutes. Scrape down sides of bowl with spatula.*

6 large eggs, lightly beaten

1 orange, zested*

1 teaspoon vanilla extract

} *Add eggs one at a time on low speed. (Batter may look curdled.) Scrape down sides of bowl with spatula.*

5½ cups unbleached all-purpose flour

2½ teaspoons baking powder

1 teaspoon salt

} *Combine and slowly add to bowl on low speed until smooth, about 2 to 3 minutes.*

1 bag (12 ounces) dark chocolate chips*

2 cups dried cherries*

} *Stir in.*

Shape 4 (2-inch x 14-inch) logs on parchment paper lined baking sheets (2 on each sheet, 3-inches apart).

1 egg yolk mixed with 1 teaspoon water

} *Brush on logs.*

2 tablespoons sugar

} *Sprinkle on logs.*

Bake 15 to 20 minutes or until lightly golden.

Loosen cookie logs using offset metal spatula underneath. Slice on a diagonal into ½-inch slices using sharp serrated knife while cookie strip is still warm. Turn cookies on their side and bake an additional 10 to 12 minutes or until lightly golden.

TIPS:

*Substitute chocolate and cherries with 4 cups whole unsalted almonds or your favorite nut and omit the orange zest.

Recipe can be halved.

These biscotti last one month in airtight container or freeze beautifully up to two months.

Makes about 5 Dozen Biscotti

Another recipe I found tucked away in a frayed envelope handwritten by my Grandmother I changed it up a little to make it chewy yet not dry. It's just perfect to dunk in your favorite hot beverage or after dinner cordial. We prefer either an espresso or a dry robust red wine or port.

Halloween

Halloween

Surprise Chili *with* Frightful Toppings

Basmati Fusion Rice

Cider Infused Hot Dogs

Ghoulish Cinnamon Glazed Sauerkraut *with*
Caramelized Onions and Apples

Frightful Trifle

Chocolate Chip Cookie Dough

Spider Web Chocolate Chip Cookie Pizza

Orange Glazed Pumpkin Bundt Cake

Caramel Dipped Apples

Two-Toned Candy Corn Cupcakes

Bugful Crispy Treats

Great for a crowd, but beware, goblins may come and devour it all.

Surprise Chili *with* Frightful Toppings

2 tablespoons extra virgin olive oil

4 celery stalks, chopped

4 carrots, chopped

1 large onion, chopped

1 red pepper, chopped

3 cloves garlic, chopped

Heat large skillet on medium high heat. Add and heat olive oil. Add remaining ingredients and cook until tender, about 5 minutes. Add to large stockpot.

8 pounds meatloaf mixture (ground veal, pork and beef)

Brown in large skillet and add to vegetables.

2 cans (28 ounces each) chopped tomatoes, undrained

4 tablespoons chili powder

1 tablespoon chipotle chili powder

1 tablespoon cumin

Salt and pepper

Add to meat and vegetables. Cook over medium heat, stirring occasionally, 45 minutes. This can be kept on low heat for a few hours before serving. The flavors will develop even better.

Serve chili with shredded cheddar cheese, shredded lettuce, chopped tomato, beans, sour cream, chopped cilantro, chopped scallions and/or chopped avocado for frightful toppings.

Makes about 32 Servings

TIPS:

Can be made one or two days ahead to marry flavors. Keep refrigerated, then just heat and serve.

Recipe can be halved.

A wonderful complement to chili and it has a natural nuttiness.

Basmati Fusion Rice

2 tablespoons extra virgin olive oil
2 tablespoons butter

} *Heat over medium high heat in 3-quart saucepan.*

2 shallots, chopped
2 cups Basmati brown rice

} *Add and cook, stirring constantly, about 3 minutes or until lightly browned.*

4½ cups Chicken Stock* (see page 96)
½ teaspoon cinnamon
¼ teaspoon ground nutmeg
Salt and pepper

} *Add and bring to a boil.*

Cover and simmer over low heat, 45 minutes or until rice is done.

Sprinkle, if desired, with chopped scallions.

Makes 6 Cups Rice, about 12 Servings

TIPS:

*Can substitute store bought chicken broth.

Browning rice first makes rice deliciously nuttier.

Cider Infused Hot Dogs

Hot dogs of your choosing
Enough cider to cover hot dogs completely

} *Bring to a boil in large stockpot. Cook, 15 minutes or until done.*

Serve with my Ghoulish Cinnamon Glazed Sauerkraut with Caramelized Onions and Apples.

TIPS:

My favorite hot dogs are Thumann's® brand.

Can also cook in a slow cooker and keep on low heat to keep hot dogs warm all night for a larger crowd.

Ghoulish Cinnamon Glazed Sauerkraut *with* Caramelized Onions and Apples

¼ cup (½ stick) butter

} *Melt in large skillet on medium heat.*

1 large Vidalia onion, thinly sliced
2 red or green apples, thinly sliced

} *Add and cook, 10 minutes or until tender.*

½ cup light brown sugar

} *Add and continue cooking until sugar is melted, stirring gently and onions and apples are lightly browned.*

2 teaspoons cinnamon
½ teaspoon nutmeg

} *Stir into mixture.*

1 package (16 ounces) sauerkraut
(rinsed and well drained)

} *Toss in and heat through.*

Makes about 16 Servings

Every year my family and I would go pumpkin picking at Ort Farms in Long Valley, N.J. Afterward, we would stop at the Hacklebarney Farms Cider Mill to get our fix of homemade apple cider and freshly made donuts. While waiting on line, they served the customers hot dogs steaming in apple cider. Here is my inspired version.

A classic death by chocolate version with a "frightful" touch.

Frightful Trifle

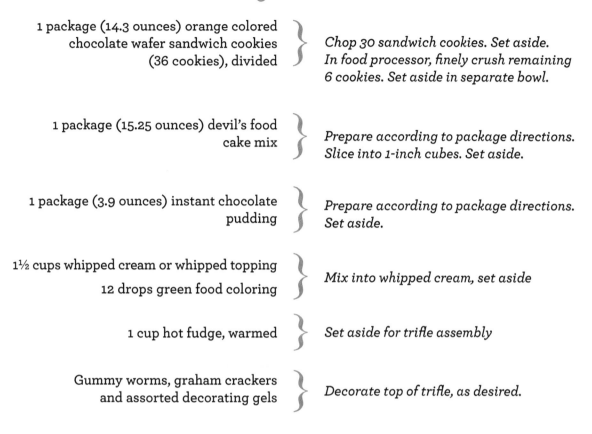

1 package (14.3 ounces) orange colored
chocolate wafer sandwich cookies
(36 cookies), divided

> Chop 30 sandwich cookies. Set aside.
> In food processor, finely crush remaining
> 6 cookies. Set aside in separate bowl.

1 package (15.25 ounces) devil's food
cake mix

> Prepare according to package directions.
> Slice into 1-inch cubes. Set aside.

1 package (3.9 ounces) instant chocolate
pudding

> Prepare according to package directions.
> Set aside.

1½ cups whipped cream or whipped topping
12 drops green food coloring

> Mix into whipped cream, set aside

1 cup hot fudge, warmed

> Set aside for trifle assembly

Gummy worms, graham crackers
and assorted decorating gels

> Decorate top of trifle, as desired.

To Assemble Trifle:

Place half of cake cubes in bottom of trifle dish or large glass serving bowl.
Drizzle with half of hot fudge, half of pudding mixture, half of chopped
sandwich cookies and half of whipped cream topping.
Repeat for second layer. Sprinkle with crushed sandwich cookies.

*Makes about
16 Servings*

TIP:

*Can be made and wrapped in refrigerator
with plastic wrap one day ahead.*

Chocolate chip cookies are classic and just irresistible in my house. Here is a perfect recipe by itself or for a cookie pizza that's fantastic for birthdays and any fun party!

Chocolate Chip Cookie Dough

Preheat oven to 350°F.

1½ cups all-purpose flour
1 ½ cups bread flour
1 teaspoon baking soda
1 teaspoon salt

Combine in medium bowl. Set aside.

1 cup (2 sticks) butter, softened
¾ cup dark brown sugar
¾ cup sugar

Combine in large bowl of electric mixer. Beat on high speed, about 3 minutes or until light and creamy.

2 eggs, slightly beaten
1 teaspoon vanilla extract

Add and beat on medium high speed, 1 minute or until combined.

1 bag (12 ounces, about 2 cups) semi-sweet or dark chocolate chips
1 cup chopped walnuts (optional)

Stir in. Chill at least 30 minutes.*

Use according to Spider Web Chocolate Chip Cookie Pizza (See page 83) or drop heaping tablespoon onto parchment-lined baking sheet, about 2-inches apart.

Bake, 8 to 10 minutes or until lightly browned.

Makes about 4 Dozen Cookies

TIPS:

*Best to chill dough before you bake. This makes a chewy center with a crispy outside. Place extra chips, before baking, onto spooned dough mounds for a pretty chocolate chip presentation.

Dough can be made ahead and frozen up to one month.

This has become a Halloween tradition that was inspired by a recipe I foodstyled for Nabisco® a long time ago. Your kids will love to help make this and pick the spiders off the web, too!

Spider Web Chocolate Chip Cookie Pizza

Preheat oven to 350°F.

*Line 9 x 13-inch baking pan with heavy-duty aluminum foil, extended
over edges of pan. Spray with non-stick cooking spray, line with parchment paper
and spray again. (Remember BPB: The butter, paper, butter rule in baking.)
This prevents Cookie Pizza from sticking to bottom of pan and create easy removal. Set aside.*

3 cups of Chocolate Chip Cookie Dough Recipe* (See page 81. NOTE: Recipe makes 6 cups dough so use remaining dough to make extra pizza, cookies or freeze for another recipe)

Press cookie dough evenly onto pizza pan. Bake, 15 minutes or until lightly browned. Let cool.

1½ cups marshmallow cream

Spread marshmallow cream on cookie cake.

2 squares (1 ounce each) semi-sweet chocolate, melted

Place in small plastic sandwich bag or piping bag. With scissor, cut small opening at end. Drizzle chocolate in circular pattern on marshmallow cream. Drag small knife, toothpick or metal spatula from center outward going back and forth to make spider web.

Cookie Spiders** (see below)

Decorate with Cookie Spiders.

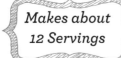

*Makes about
12 Servings*

TIPS:

*Can substitute with refrigerated cookie dough.

**Spider Cookies: Cut black string licorice into 1½-inch pieces. Insert 8 pieces into orange colored chocolate sandwich cookies to resemble spider legs. Attach red hot cinnamon candies with melted chocolate to make eyes.

Orange Glazed Pumpkin Bundt Cake

Preheat oven to 350°F.

Spray pumpkin cake pan molds or two 8-inch bundt pans generously with non-stick cooking spray, (or rub with softened butter and dust with flour). Set aside.

Pumpkin Bundt Cake:

1 package (15.25 ounces) yellow cake mix

3 large eggs

½ cup vegetable oil

1 can (15 ounces) pumpkin puree

1 tablespoon pumpkin spice*

Combine in large bowl of electric mixer. Beat on high speed, 2 minutes.

Pour into prepared pan(s). Bake, 40 minutes or until toothpick inserted in center tests clean. Let cool.

4 ounces (½ brick) cream cheese

¼ cup (½ stick) butter

1 ½ cups confectioner's sugar

Combine in large bowl of electric mixer. Beat on high speed, about 5 minutes or until smooth.

To assemble cake, place bottom half on serving plate. Top with cream cheese mixture and spread evenly. Top with second half of pumpkin cake.

Orange Glaze:

2 cups confectioner's sugar

1 orange, zested, and
1 tablespoon orange juice

4 drops orange food coloring (or 3 yellow drops and 2 red drops food coloring to make orange)

Combine in small bowl with wire whisk. Drizzle onto cake.

Assorted cake decorations
(sprinkles and candies)

Decorate with icing, colored sprinkles and any other desired candies.

TIPS:

*Can substitute pumpkin pie spice with 1 teaspoon cinnamon, ½ teaspoon nutmeg, ½ teaspoon ginger, and ¼ teaspoon allspice.

Can make cake three days ahead and store in refrigerator or freeze up to one month.

Let the kids decorate as they desire!

Makes about 16 Servings

A sweet surprise after trick-or-treating or centerpiece for your table.

Caramel Dipped Apples

1 package (11 ounces) caramels

Melt caramels according to package directions.

4 apples
4 wooden popsticks*

Wash and dry apples thoroughly so caramel adheres to them.

Place wooden popstick into stems of each apple.

Dip apples according to package directions.

Topping suggestions:

Assorted nuts, chopped

Chocolate or orange-colored sandwich cookies, chopped

Pretzels, chopped

Decorative sprinkles

Mini marshmallows

Candy bars, chopped

Flaked coconut

Candy corn

Candy coated chocolates

White, dark or milk chocolate, melted

Dip apples in desired toppings and then drizzle with melted chocolates.

Makes 4 Caramel Apples

TIPS:

Substitute wooden popsticks with cinnamon sticks for a festive look!

Have each finished caramel apple placed on individual parchment covered paper plates so kids can easily bring them home after they dip them.

My daughters loved unwrapping the caramels the night before our big Halloween party every year with family and friends since it made them even more excited for the festivities to come. Have the kids make their own and they'll love them even more. Use these suggested toppings or have fun coming up with your own.

The cutest cupcakes for Halloween lovers at any age.

Two-Toned Candy Corn Cupcakes

Preheat oven to 350°F.

Place decorative cupcake cups into muffin tins. Set aside.

1 box (15.25 ounces) white cake mix

Food coloring (follow directions to make orange color)

2 teaspoons orange extract

Prepare cake mix in mixing bowl according to package directions using whole eggs. Stir in orange extract and food coloring. Spoon batter evenly into muffin cups. Bake, 20 minutes or until done. Let cool.

1 cup white canned frosting

1 cup orange decorating icing

Decorative sprinkles and candy corn

*Spoon white and orange frostings, alternating, into pastry bag fitted with star tip. Use to pipe frosting onto cupcakes. Decorate with Halloween sprinkles and candy corn.

Makes 24 Cupcakes

TIPS:

*This will create a two-tone look.

Pipe icing in pastry bag with large star tip for decorative and professional-looking tops.

Bugful Crispy Treats

Line 9 x 13-inch baking pan with aluminum foil.
Spray with non-stick cooking spray. Line bottom with parchment paper
and spray again. (Remember BPB: The butter, paper, butter rule.)
This prevents treats from sticking to bottom of pan and create easy removal. Set aside.

1 bag (12 ounces) marshmallows

3 tablespoons butter

Combine in 1-quart heatproof measuring cup or casserole dish. Heat in microwave, 1 minute and 30 seconds. Stir and heat additional 30 seconds or until melted.

8 cups crisp rice cereal

Combine in large bowl with melted marshmallow mixture. Stir quickly with wet spatula.

Place mixture into prepared pan with wet hands. Quickly smooth top with bottom of metal measuring cup dipped in water. Let cool and cut into squares.

Assorted sprinkles

Gummy worms, assorted gummy treats and googly eyes.

Top with Halloween sprinkles and, if desired, gummy treats.

Makes 24 Squares

TIPS:

Can be made, wrapped with plastic wrap and stored in refrigerator three days ahead.

I usually make 3 batches and use a 12½ x 17½ x 1-inch half sheet pan for a big crowd.

I make these marshmallow treats extra thick and gooey with gummy worms for a dreadful treat.

Thanksgiving

Thanksgiving

Chicken Stock

Escarole Soup *with* Mini Meatballs
and Parmesan Egg Battered Croutons

Savory Roasted Herb Turkey *with* Wild Mushroom Gravy

Roasted Brussels Sprouts *with* Pancetta, Shallots and Fig Jam

Sausage, Apple and Herb Stuffing *with*
Roasted Chestnuts and Cranberries

Creamy Whipped Baked Mashed Potatoes

Sweet Potato Gratin Topped *with* Vanilla Marshmallows

Cornbread Pudding

Fresh Cranberry Orange Relish

Pumpkin Cheesecake *with* Gingersnap Crust

Flakey Pie Pastry Dough for Single Crust

Harvest Pumpkin Pie

Chocolate Bourbon Pecan Pie

Flakey Pie Pastry Dough for Double Crust

Apple Pear Pie

Cranberry Cheesecake Crumb Pie

Pear Galette *with* Apricot Glaze

Pumpkin Crème Brûlée

Chicken Stock

Bouquet Garni Sachet*:

3 bay leaves

2 sprigs each of fresh thyme, rosemary and sage

½ bunch Italian parsley sprigs

10 peppercorns

6 whole cloves

8-inch piece of cheesecloth

Butcher string

Place in center of cheesecloth. Tie ends together with butcher string to make bundle. Set aside.

Stock:

4 quarts water

1 chicken (3 pound whole or cut up), skin removed

1 large Vidalia onion, peeled

1 large tomato

1 leek, trimmed and cleaned

4 large carrots, peeled

4 celery ribs, peeled

6 cloves garlic, peeled

Prepared Bouquet Garni Sachet

Add to large stockpot. Bring to a boil. Immediately reduce to medium low heat. Simmer, 2 hours or until chicken pulls apart easily. NOTE: Skim foam from surface occasionally to get rid of any impurities.

Strain solids using a colander with a second stockpot underneath to catch stock. Then, strain again through fine stainless steel sieve. Season with salt and pepper, as desired. Remove chicken from bones and use for soup, but discard all vegetables.

Chicken Stock is the base of all good cooking! Having it on hand in your freezer is a must. It's so easy to make and so healthy. This recipe makes quite a bit and will last a while for homemade soups and entrees. Your dishes will taste incredible with this classic base of flavor.

TIPS:

*Bouquet Garni: A bundle of herbs tied together by a string to flavor stocks and sauces. I make a sachet bundle with a cheesecloth by placing my herbs into it and then tying the bundle with butcher string. Use any combination you like. All the herbs are able to stay together and infuse the stock with many aromatic flavors.

Stock can be made ahead and frozen in plastic containers up to three months. Perfect for rice, risotto, soups and sauces.

Escarole Soup *with* Mini Meatballs and Parmesan Egg Battered Croutons

Soup:

1 onion, chopped

2 celery stalks, chopped

2 carrots, peeled and chopped

2 shallots, chopped

4 cloves garlic, chopped

¼ cup extra virgin olive oil

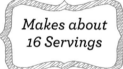

Makes about 16 Servings

Cook on medium high heat in large stockpot, 5 minutes or until tender.

8 cups Chicken Stock or water (see page 94)

2 pounds boneless, skinless chicken breasts

Add. Bring to a boil. Lower heat and simmer, 2 hours. Skim any foam from top of surface during cooking.

Salt and pepper

Season broth to taste.

Mini Meatballs:

1½ pounds meatloaf mixture (ground veal, pork and beef)*

2 eggs

½ cup fresh breadcrumbs (Italian or Semolina bread, processed in food processor until fine)**

¼ cup grated Parmesan cheese

¼ cup grated Pecorino Romano cheese

1 bunch Italian parsley, stems removed, chopped (about 1 cup)

Salt and pepper

Preheat oven to 350°F (if baking meatballs in oven.)

Mix in large bowl. Roll into ¾ to 1-inch balls. (Makes about 120 to 150 mini meatballs. depending upon who is doing the rolling.)

Cook in medium saucepan with extra chicken broth, 10 minutes or until done. Remove and set aside.
Alternate oven baking method:
Place meatballs on parchment-lined baking sheet drizzled with olive oil. Bake for 15 minutes or until internal temperature reaches 160°F.

1 big bunch escarole, sliced into bite size pieces

1 box (12 ounces) orzo pasta, prepared according to package directions and drained

Remove chicken from large stockpot and shred. Add meatballs, shredded chicken, orzo and escarole to stockpot. Simmer, about 5 minutes or until escarole is soft.

*Serve with homemade croutons** and extra grated Parmesan and Pecorino Romano cheese.*

TIPS:

*Can substitute ground turkey for meatloaf mixture.

**Can substitute with Panko or plain dried breadcrumbs.

***Homemade Croutons (Our Italian Dumplings):

4 eggs
½ cup grated Parmesan cheese
½ cup grated Pecorino Romano cheese
Salt and pepper

Combine in medium bowl.

1 large loaf semolina bread, cut into ½-inch cubes, lightly toasted

Toss in egg mixture.

Extra virgin olive oil (for frying)

Pour into large heavy or cast iron skillet, about ¼-inch deep. Add dipped bread on medium high heat in single layer. Cook croutons, stirring occasionally, about 5 minutes or until golden. Drain on paper towels.

Serve with soup.

TIPS:

*** Croutons can also be baked. Place on parchment-lined baking sheet drizzled with olive oil. Bake at 400°F, 20 minutes, stirring occasionally or until golden brown and crisp.

Can make croutons one day ahead and heat in oven to crisp up at 350°F for 10 minutes.

The origin of Italian Wedding Soup actually comes from the Italian name "Minestra Maritata" which translates to "Married Soup" for marrying the flavors. We traditionally enjoy it during the holidays such as Thanksgiving and Christmas. Enjoy this soup anytime with family and friends. Complete comfort during any cold, winter night as well.

Savory Roasted Herb Turkey *with* Wild Mushroom Gravy

Savory Roasted Herb Turkey:

1 (12 to 14 pounds) fresh turkey

1 cup (2 sticks) butter, softened

2 (4-inch) sprigs rosemary, leaves removed, chopped slightly

1 small bunch sage, reserve 6 leaves, chop remaining

3 to 4 sprigs thyme, leaves removed

4 cloves garlic, finely chopped

Salt and pepper

2 apples, halved

2 onions, halved

4 cloves garlic

4 celery stalks

4 large carrots, peeled and cut into large chunks

2 sprigs rosemary

2 sprigs sage

2 sprigs thyme

Salt and pepper

Preheat oven to 425°F.

Clean and pat dry.
Place on roasting rack in roasting pan.

Combine in small bowl and mix well. Separate skin from turkey breast with fingertips. Rub half of herb mixture underneath skin, being careful not to tear skin. Place reserved 6 sage leaves under skin for decoration. Rub remaining herb mixture all over outside surface of skin.

Place one-half apple and one-half onion into bird cavity. Place one-half apple and one-half onion in front breast cavity. Tuck skin over to make smooth front. Add remaining ingredients in roasting pan.

Bake 10 minutes. Cover loosely with foil. Reduce oven to 350°F for 3 to 4 hours or 25 minutes per pound, basting every 30 minutes.

Take foil off when turkey reaches 160°F. Bake additional 20 minutes or until browned and meat thermometer reaches 175°F in breast and 180°F in thigh. Allow to sit at least 30 minutes before carving.

TIP:

TURKEY STOCK: To make turkey stock, place turkey neck in medium saucepan filled with 6 cups of water and additional rosemary, sage and thyme, onion, celery and carrots. Simmer while turkey is cooking, about 2 hours. Use this broth to flavor stuffing while baking and to make the gravy.

Makes 16 to 20 Servings

This turkey comes out so beautifully, it will be a showpiece for your holiday celebration. Decorate the turkey platter with fresh herbs, clementines and fresh cranberries for a beautiful centerpiece before carving. I always make two smaller turkeys. They cook faster and are moister because you will not overcook them as much as a bigger bird. There will be plenty of white and dark meat to go around, too.

Wild Mushroom Gravy:

½ cup (1 stick) butter
2 shallots, chopped
2 cloves garlic, chopped

Melt butter in medium saucepan. Add shallots and garlic and cook on medium heat until fragrant, about 3 minutes.

½ cup all-purpose flour
1 package (12 ounces) assorted wild mushrooms, sliced, about 3 cups

Add to saucepan. Continue to cook about 3 to 5 minutes, stirring constantly until mushrooms are soft.

¼ cup white wine or sherry
Combination of fresh rosemary, sage and thyme, chopped (about 2 tablespoons)

Add to saucepan and stir thoroughly.

Turkey drippings from roasting pan and enough Chicken Stock or Turkey Stock to make 2 cups (see page 98)

Whisk in saucepan. Bring to a boil, then simmer until thickened. Salt and pepper to taste.

Makes about 3 Cups Gravy

TIP:

Can make after turkey is done.

Cover surface with plastic wrap placed directly on top to prevent skin from forming.

Keep refrigerated if serving more than one hour before dinner. Just reheat right before serving.

"My daughters and I carving the holiday turkeys".

This velvety savory gravy topped over your sliced turkey will add the finishing touch to your incredible Thanksgiving feast.

Brussels sprouts seem
to be the most misunderstood
vegetable. My husband never liked
them until I made this version.
This recipe will become a favorite
for Brussels sprouts lovers
and skeptics alike.

Roasted Brussels Sprouts *with* Pancetta, Shallots and Fig Jam

Preheat oven to 450°F.

2 pounds (about 8 cups) Brussels sprouts, quartered

4 ounces chopped pancetta

½ cup extra virgin olive oil

2 tablespoons butter

1 jar (8.5 ounces) fig jam

2 to 4 tablespoons fig vinegar (or any fruity vinegar)

Salt and pepper

Toss in shallow roasting pan or on baking sheet.

Bake, stirring occasionally, 25 to 35 minutes or until crisp and golden.

Makes 8 to 10 Servings

TIPS:

Make sure Brussels sprouts are crisp and golden with slightly browned edges. Browning will give them extra flavor and a natural sweetness.

Recipe can be easily doubled or halved.

To make it extra healthy and colorful, add 1 pound cubed butternut squash, if desired, and cook as above.

This is my most requested Thanksgiving recipe. This stuffing will make your turkey proud! It's also a terrific stuffing for a pork roast.

Sausage, Apple and Herb Stuffing *with* Roasted Chestnuts and Cranberries

Makes about 30 Servings

1 loaf Challah bread (1 pound), cut into 1-inch cubes (about 16 cups)

1 loaf Italian or Semolina bread (1 pound), cut into 1-inch cubes (about 12 cups)

1 cup (2 sticks) butter, melted

½ cup (1 stick) butter

2 large Vidalia or sweet onions, chopped

4 shallots, chopped

4 sticks celery, chopped

4 large carrots, chopped

4 cloves garlic, finely chopped

3 tart apples (Granny Smith, Macintosh, or combination of both), seeded and chopped (leave skin on for color)

2 pounds bulk Italian sweet sausage

Combination of fresh herbs, rosemary, sage, thyme (handful of each, slightly chopped)

1 bunch Italian parsley, stems removed and chopped (about 1 cup)

3 to 4 cups Chicken Stock or Turkey Stock (see page 98). Stuffing should be moist, not soggy. Can always add more during cooking.

Salt and pepper (This is very important. Make sure you taste to see if it is necessary.)

2 cups dried cranberries

2 cups cooked Roasted Chestnuts, chopped (optional)**

Preheat oven to 375°F.

Place bread cubes on baking sheets and drizzle with butter. Bake until crisp and golden, stirring occasionally, 10 to 15 minutes. Put in large bowl.

Reduce oven to 350°F.

Melt butter in medium skillet on medium heat. Add and cook remaining ingredients until tender, about 10 minutes. Add mixture to same bowl above with toasted bread cubes.

Add and cook on medium high heat in same skillet. Do not drain. Add to same bowl with bread/vegetable mixture.

Sprinkle mixture with herbs and drizzle with chicken broth or stock until moistened.

Stir into mixture. Place prepared stuffing in greased large deep (3 to 4-quart) baking dish or baking pan.

Bake, 25 minutes, drizzling with either your turkey drippings and/or Chicken Stock/ Turkey Stock to keep moistened. Using the juices of roasted Turkey Stock gives stuffing the same awesome savory flavor that matches stuffing cooked inside a turkey. Cover with foil if it gets too browned, but I love the crispy burnt parts!

TIPS:

*Can substitute Chicken Stock or Turkey Stock with store-bought boxed Chicken Broth.

**For Roasted Chestnuts: make an "X" with paring knife about ¼-inch deep into center of flat side of chestnuts. Place on baking sheet and splash with about 2 tablespoons water. Bake at 425°F until chestnuts start to open, about 25 minutes. Let cool. Peel and chop for stuffing.

I prefer to not stuff the turkey because it cooks more evenly and prevents undercooking or overcooking.

Stuffing can be made one to two days ahead (do not add turkey drippings/and or turkey stock until day of serving.)

105

Creamy Whipped Baked Mashed Potatoes

Preheat oven to 350°F.

5 pounds russet potatoes,
peeled and cut into chunks

2 teaspoons salt

Boil in large pot until fork tender, about 12 to 15 minutes. Strain from hot water and immediately place into large bowl of electric mixer.

½ cup (1 stick) butter

¾ cup heavy cream or whole milk

Salt and pepper

Add to potatoes and beat on medium high speed with wire whip or paddle attachment until smooth but a little lumpy, about 2 to 3 minutes. DO NOT OVERBEAT or potatoes will get gluey. Lumps are luscious and a sign of good, homemade mashed potatoes. Spoon into lightly buttered large casserole dish.

2 tablespoons butter, melted

1 small bunch chives
(about 2 tablespoons), snipped

Combine and brush on potatoes. Can be prepared one day ahead up to this point.

Bake 30 to 40 minutes or until top is golden brown.

Makes 15-20 Servings

TIPS:

Make sure potatoes are hot from the pot when starting to mix them with butter and cream. This will make them creamier and lighter. REMEMBER: DO NOT over mix. Some lumps are nice.

If you make ahead, place plastic wrap right on top of potatoes to prevent moisture, then chill. Let stand to room temperature before baking.

My daughters promise that these are the best mashed potatoes in the world. Although they are very rich, it's a holiday so a great time to splurge. Use the whole milk option for a less rich but equally creamy and delicious version.

My husband and both of my daughters have a significant sweet tooth. This dish always satisfies them in between the spread of savory dishes decorating the Thanksgiving table, even before dessert.

Sweet Potato Gratin Topped *with* Vanilla Marshmallows

Preheat over to 375°F.

3 pounds sweet potatoes or yams
(about 4 large)

Bake on cookie sheet, 45 to 60 minutes or until tender. Let cool.

Cut in half and scoop out center into large bowl. Mash with fork or potato masher until smooth.

¼ cup butter (½ stick), melted
¼ cup dark brown sugar
1 teaspoon ground cinnamon*
1 teaspoon ground ginger*
¼ teaspoon ground nutmeg*
Salt and pepper

Combine in medium bowl until blended. Add to potatoes. Combine until smooth. Pour into greased 2-quart deep casserole dish. Bake, 30 to 35 minutes or until heated through and a little puffy.

1 package (10 ounces) vanilla marshmallows**

Top and bake 5 minutes or until marshmallows are golden and puffed.

Makes about 12 Servings

TIPS:

*Can substitute all spices with 1 tablespoon pumpkin pie spice.

**Can substitute with regular or mini marshmallows.

Can be made one day ahead. Top with marshmallows day of serving and bake as directed above.

Recipe can be easily doubled.

Garnish with fresh sage leaves.

Cornbread Pudding

2 cans (15.25 ounces each) whole kernel corn, drained*

2 cans (14.75 ounces each) creamed corn, undrained

1 cup (2 sticks) butter, melted

1 cup (8 ounces) sour cream

4 eggs, slightly beaten

½ teaspoom nutmeg

Preheat oven to 375°F.

Combine in large bowl.

2 boxes (8.5 ounces each) corn muffin or cornbread mix

Stir into corn mixture. Pour into well-greased 4-quart casserole dish or two 2-quart casserole dishes.

2 tablespoons butter, melted

Brush on prepared pudding.

1 bunch chives (about ½ cup), snipped, optional

Top prepared pudding.

Bake, 35 to 40 minutes or until golden brown and puffed.

Makes about 16 Servings

TIPS:

Substitute with Mexican corn. Add 1 teaspoon chili powder and top with a Mexican cheese blend for a spicy twist.

If you can't wait for the next holiday to enjoy this side dish, it can be easily halved for an everyday meal. Use a 2-quart casserole dish.

This recipe was inspired by my cousin Jackie. In addition to giving it a little twist, I doubled it because the dish, will be scraped clean before all your guests have the chance to try it. You will definitely want leftovers of this dish as well.

Fresh Cranberry Orange Relish

2 oranges, zested and juiced
(about ⅔ cup juice)
2 tablespoons cornstarch

Whisk together in medium saucepan until blended.

1 bag (12 ounces) fresh cranberries
(about 4 cups)*
1 cup sugar
2 cinnamon sticks

Add to saucepan and stir until blended. Bring to a boil and cook on medium heat, stirring occasionally, about 5 minutes or until thickened and cranberries are slightly crushed. Place in large bowl. Cover with plastic wrap. Chill. Remove cinnamon sticks before serving.

Makes about 1½ Cups

TIPS:

*Can substitute with frozen cranberries, thawed.

A perfect accompaniment for pork roast, too.

Recipe can be made two days ahead and is easily doubled.

Garnish with additional orange zest.

The orange marries the cranberries perfectly for a sweet citrus side dish.

Pumpkin Cheesecake *with* Gingersnap Crust

Preheat oven to 350°F.

Place shallow baking pan in lower rack of oven (half sheet pan works perfectly). Fill with at least 1-inch water. The moisture from the steam helps prevent the cheesecake from cracking.

Open springform pan. Insert the bottom pan upside down and close springform pan.
Line 9-inch springform pan with circle of parchment paper.
This method allows your cheesecake to slide right off onto your serving plate much easier.
Wrap outside of springform with heavy-duty aluminum foil to prevent
any seeping of butter through pan when baking.

Crust:

2 cups finely crushed ginger snaps, (about 36 cookies)

¼ cup light brown sugar

6 tablespoons butter, melted

1 teaspoon cinnamon

Combine in medium bowl.
Press firmly into bottom of springform pan.
Bake, 10 minutes. Cool.

Batter:

4 packages (8 ounces each) cream cheese, softened

¾ cup sugar

¾ cup light brown sugar

Beat in large bowl of electric mixer on high speed until light and fluffy, about 5 minutes.

1 cup canned pumpkin

Add and beat on medium speed until smooth.

3 tablespoons all-purpose flour

½ cup sour cream

Add and beat on low speed until smooth, about 1 minute.

3 eggs

Add one at a time and beat on low speed until blended, about 1 minute. DO NOT OVERBEAT. (This also helps prevent cheesecake from cracking.)

1 tablespoon cinnamon

1 tablespoon pumpkin pie spice*

1 teaspoon vanilla extract

¼ teaspoon salt

Add and beat on low speed until smooth, about 30 seconds. Pour into prepared pan. Place on middle rack of oven. Bake 1 hour and 30 minutes or until center is almost set. Let cool.

Chill, 2 hours or overnight.

114

The gingersnap crust adds a tangy heat, complementing the creaminess and subtleness of the fall's classic pumpkin.

Topping:

1 cup sour cream

¼ cup confectioner's sugar

1 teaspoon pumpkin pie spice

1 teaspoon cinnamon

Combine and top cheesecake. Spread almost to edge. Keep refrigerated until serving.

TIPS:

*Can substitute pumpkin pie spice with 1 teaspoon cinnamon, ½ teaspoon nutmeg, ½ teaspoon ginger and ¼ teaspoon allspice.

Cheesecake freezes beautifully. Can be made, cooled then frozen up to three weeks ahead. Just add topping after defrosting.

Makes about 16 Servings

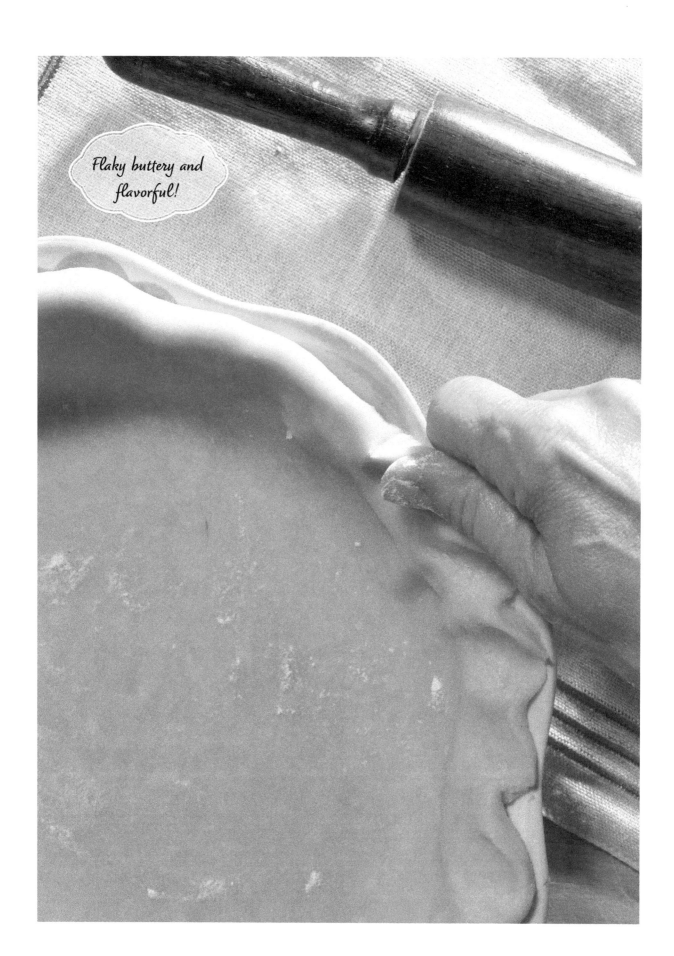

Flakey Pie Pastry Dough for Single Crust

1¾ cups all-purpose flour

½ teaspoon salt

Combine in food processor and pulse two to three times.

¾ cup (1½ sticks) chilled unsalted butter, cut up into ½-inch cubes

Add to food processor and pulse until flour looks like small peas. (DO NOT OVER PROCESS. This will cause butter to melt and make dough tough).

4 to 5 tablespoons Ice Water or more, if needed

(Ice Water: Place a few ice cubes in ½ cup of water)

Slowly add and pulse several times until dough JUST comes together when squeezed. If the dough falls apart, and 2 to 4 more tablespoons of ice water and pulse a couple of times until it JUST starts to form a ball. Wrap in plastic wrap. Chill, 15 minutes. Let sit at room temperature 5 to 10 minutes before rolling.

Lightly flour surface, top of dough and rolling pin. Roll dough gently to 10-inch circle, about ⅛-inch thick.

Lightly dust 9 to 10-inch pie plate with flour. Gently place rolled pastry onto floured pie plate.

Press into pie plate. Flute edge by pinching pastry dough between thumb and forefinger to crimp.

*Brush with Egg Wash. Freeze prepared pie plate 10 minutes before baking, to prevent the crimped edges from shrinking during baking.

NOTE: Use directions above for recipes calling for UNBAKED pie pastry.

NOTE: Use directions below for recipes calling for BAKED pie pastry.

Preheat oven to 425°F.

Poke the sides and bottom of the pastry dough with tines of fork 12 times.

Brush pastry dough with Egg Wash.*

Bake, 10 to 15 minutes or until golden.

Let cool before filling.

Makes 1 Single Crust

TIPS:

*EGG WASH: Mix 1 egg yolk with 1 teaspoon water. Brush on pastry dough before baking for golden glow.

Pastry dough can be made two days ahead and kept wrapped in refrigerator. Also, freezes beautifully up to one month.

Can freeze dough whole, wrapped in plastic wrap. Or, press it into pie plate, wrap in plastic wrap, and freeze up to one month. Then, it's ready to be filled and baked easily!

This recipe is a pumpkin lover's delight and quick to make. Use my homemade pie crust recipe for an added touch of holiday warmth.

Harvest Pumpkin Pie

Preheat oven to 425°F.

1 can (15 ounces) pumpkin (about 1¾ cups)

½ cup brown sugar

½ cup granulated sugar

2 eggs, lightly beaten

2 teaspoon cinnamon

1 teaspoon nutmeg

½ teaspoon all spice

½ teaspoon ginger

½ teaspoon salt

Combine in large bowl.

1 cup heavy cream

Whisk into pumpkin mixture.

Flakey Pie Pastry Dough for Single Crust*
(see page 117)

Press into 9-inch pie plate. Flute edge by pinching pastry between thumb and forefinger to crimp.

**Brush with Egg Wash. Freeze 10 minutes before adding pumpkin mixture, to prevent the crimped edges from shrinking during baking.

Fill with pumpkin mixture.

Bake 10 minutes. Reduce heat to 350°F, continue to bake 40 to 45 minutes or until set in center. Cover pie loosely with aluminum foil if crust gets too brown during baking. Let cool. Refrigerate until serving if serving next day.

Serve, if desired, with fresh whipped cream or favorite whipped topping.

TIPS:

*Can substitute Flakey Pie Pastry Dough for Single Crust recipe with store-bought prepared refrigerated pie crust.

Roll out scraps of extra pastry dough and use small festive cookie cutters to cut out shapes to decorate top of pie. Place on pie before baking.

**EGG WASH: Mix 1 egg yolk with 1 teaspoon water. Brush on pastry dough edges after filling before baking for golden glow.

*Makes
12 Servings*

Chocolate Bourbon Pecan Pie

Preheat oven to 375°F.

½ cup sugar

½ cup dark corn syrup

¼ cup (½ stick) butter, melted

2 eggs, lightly beaten   *Combine in medium bowl.*

¼ cup bourbon or rum

1 teaspoon vanilla extract

½ teaspoon salt

8 ounces semi-sweet chocolate, (any good quality chocolate), chopped and melted   *Add and stir into corn syrup mixture until well combined.*

Flakey Pie Pastry Dough for Single Crust* (see page 117)   *Press into 9-inch pie plate and flute edge by pinching pastry between thumb and forefinger to crimp.*

Makes 12 Servings

**Brush with Egg Wash. Freeze 10 minutes before adding pie mixture, to prevent the crimped edges from shrinking during baking.

1 package (8 ounces) pecan halves (about 1½ cups)   *Fill with pie mixture.*

Top filling mixture. Place in circular pattern with round side facing up.

TIPS:

*Can substitute Flakey Pie Pastry Dough for Single Crust recipe with store-bought prepared refrigerated pie crust.

**EGG WASH: Mix 1 egg yolk with 1 teaspoon water. Brush on pastry dough edges after filling before baking for golden glow.

Bake, 50 to 55 minutes or until done. Cover pie loosely with aluminum foil if pie crust gets too brown during baking.

Let cool. Refrigerate until serving if serving next day.

Serve, if desired, with fresh whipped cream or favorite whipped topping.

A twist on traditional pecan pie with the addition of rich chocolate. Bourbon or rum gives it an impressive kick, too.

This is a very stable dough and is not as fragile as a traditional one. I have experimented throughout my food styling career to make a crust that holds up perfectly and tastes magnificent.

Flakey Pie Pastry Dough for Double Crust

4 cups all-purpose flour, sifted

2 tablespoons sugar

1 teaspoon salt

} *Combine in food processor and pulse two to three times.*

1 cup chilled shortening (white or butter flavor)

¼ cup (½ stick) chilled, unsalted butter, cut up into ½-inch cubes

} *Add and pulse until flour looks like small peas. (DO NOT OVER PROCESS. This will cause butter to melt and make pastry tough).*

8 to 10 tablespoons Ice Water or more, if needed (Ice Water: Place a few ice cubes in 1 cup of water)

1 egg, beaten

1 tablespoon fresh lemon juice

} *Slowly add and pulse several times until dough JUST forms a ball. Add more ice water, one tablespoon at a time, if needed, to hold dough together. Divide into 2 even doughs.*

Wrap each individually in plastic wrap. Chill, 20 minutes. Let sit at room temperature 5 to 10 minutes befor rolling.

On floured surface, roll each pastry dough gently to 10-inch circle, about ⅛-inch thick.

Lightly dust 9 to 10-inch pie plate with flour. Gently place one rolled pastry dough onto floured pie plate. Press into pie plate. Flute edge by pinching pastry dough between thumb and forefinger to crimp.

Continue with second pastry dough according to Apple Pear Pie recipe (see page 125).

Makes 2 (9 to 10-inch) Pie Crusts

TIPS:

Pie dough can be made two days ahead and kept wrapped in refrigerator. Also, freezes beautifully up to one month. I usually roll dough, press it into pie plate, wrap in plastic wrap and freeze it. For second dough, I roll it out on parchment-lined cookie sheet, wrap in plastic wrap and freeze it. It's ready to go anytime!

The combination of apples and pears makes this pie sweeter, more flavorful and absolutely delectable, especially when served warm with vanilla ice cream.

Apple Pear Pie

10 cups Granny Smith or Honeycrisp apples, (or combination of both, about 8 apples), cut into thick slices

Preheat oven to 400°F.

4 cups Anjou pears, (about 3 large), cut into thick slices

Combine in large bowl.

2 lemons, zested and juiced

Makes 12 Servings

⅓ cup all-purpose flour
¼ cup sugar
1 tablespoon cinnamon
½ teaspoon salt

Combine and toss with apples and pears.

Flaky Pie Pastry Dough for Double Crust* (see page 123)

Press one pastry dough into lightly floured 10-inch pie plate. Flute edge by pinching pastry between thumb and forefinger to crimp.

Fill with pie mixture.

¼ cup butter, cut into cubes

Dot fruit mixture with butter. Top with second pastry dough. Seal and flute edge by pinching pastry between thumb and forefinger to crimp.

***Brush entire pie with Egg Wash. Freeze 10 minutes before baking, to prevent crimped edges from shrinking during baking.*

1 tablespoon sugar
¼ teaspoon cinnamon

Mix and sprinkle onto entire pastry. Make several slits in pastry with tip of small knife in decorative pattern.

TIPS:

Can substitute Flakey Pie Pastry Dough for Double Crust recipe with store-bought prepared refrigerated pie crust.

Use small cookie cutters to cut out shapes from pastry scraps and decorate top of pie before baking.

***EGG WASH: Mix 1 egg yolk with 1 teaspoon water. Brush on pastry dough for golden glow.*

Can freeze unbaked pie two weeks ahead. Bake frozen pie at 375°F, cover loosely with aluminum foil, 30 minutes. Remove foil. Increase oven to 425°F. Bake 30 minutes, until browned and fruit is tender.

Place on baking sheet. Bake, 1 hour or until golden brown and fruit is tender. (Test with wooden skewer). Cover pie loosely with aluminum foil if pie crust gets too brown during baking.

Let sit 1 to 2 hours to absorb juices before serving.

Let cool. Refrigerate if serving next day.

Serve warm, if desired, with vanilla ice cream.

Cranberry Cheesecake Crumb Pie

Crust:

2 sleeves graham crackers,
finely crushed (about 2¾ cups)

1 tablespoon sugar

1 teaspoon cinnamon

¾ cup butter (1½ sticks), melted

Preheat oven to 325°F.

Combine in bowl Press into bottom and sides of 9 to 10-inch pie plate. Bake, 5 minutes. Cool.

Batter:

2 packages (8 ounces) cream cheese, softened

½ cup sugar

Zest of one lemon

1 teaspoon vanilla extract

Beat in large bowl of electric mixer on high speed until light and fluffy, about 5 minutes.

2 eggs

½ cup sour cream

Add to batter. Beat on low speed until smooth, about 1 minute. Pour into prepared crust. Bake, 20 minutes.

Makes about 10 Servings

Topping:

1½ cups Zested Cranberry
Orange Relish (see page 112)*

Top with cranberry sauce in even layer.

½ cup all- purpose flour

½ cup oats

¼ cup light brown sugar

¼ cup sugar

1 teaspoon cinnamon

½ teaspoon salt

Combine in medium bowl.

½ cup butter (1 stick), melted

Add to topping. Combine to make large and medium crumbles. Sprinkle on top of cranberry layer.

Bake, additional 20 to 25 minutes or until center is set. Loosely cover with foil last 10 minutes to prevent over browning.

Let cool. Chill at least 2 hours.

TIPS:

*Substitute Zesty Cranberry Orange Relish with 1 can (14 ounces) whole cranberry sauce, 1 tablespoon cornstarch, 1 teaspoon sugar and zest of one orange.

Can be made two days ahead.

126

This became the pie that was enjoyed to the last crumb on my dessert table. The combination of a cookie crust and cheesecake bottom topped with a cranberry and crumb topping is a sure winner!

Pear Galette *with* Apricot Glaze

Preheat oven to 425°F.

1 ¾ cups all-purpose flour

½ teaspoon salt

Combine in food processor.

¾ cup chilled unsalted butter,
cut up into ½-inch cubes

Add and pulse until flour looks like small peas. (DO NOT OVER PROCESS. This will cause butter to melt and make pastry tough).

4 to 5 tablespoons ice water

(Ice Water: Place a few ice cubes
in ½ cup of water)

Slowly add and pulse several times until dough JUST forms a ball. Add more ice water, one tablespoon at a time, if needed to hold dough together.

Wrap in plastic wrap. Chill, 20 minutes. Allow to soften at room temperature before rolling.

**Makes about
10 Servings**

Place dough between 2 pieces of large parchment paper. Roll to ⅛-inch thick and about 14-inches round. Using bottom sheet for support, transfer dough on parchment paper to large unrimmed baking sheet. Chill, at least 15 minutes. Remove parchment paper after chilling.

2 tablespoons apricot preserves

4 cups Anjou or Forelle pears,
cut into thin slices (about 3 large)

Spread preserves on pastry dough and layer slices in concentric circles leaving 1½-inch border.

2 tablespoons sugar

Zest of one lemon

Sprinkle over pear slices.

Using parchment to support dough, fold pastry border edges up and over pears, about 1½-2 inches.

2 tablespoons apricot preserves

1 tablespoon sugar

Brush preserves on pastry and pears. Sprinkle with sugar. Chill 15 minutes.

TIPS:

*Bake, 20 minutes.
Reduce oven temperature to 375°F. Bake 20 more minutes or until golden.*

Dough can be made two days ahead, wrapped in plastic wrap and refrigerated.

Dough freezes beautifully up to one month. I roll dough on parchment-lined baking sheet, wrap in plastic wrap, and freeze it. It's ready to go anytime!

Loosen galette underneath using large offset metal spatula. Let stand 10 minutes and cut into wedges. Serve warm or at room temperature. Serve with fresh whipped cream or vanilla ice cream.

I learned this rustic gorgeous tart
a long time ago when I studied in Paris.
It is so simple and you will make this often
for your guests. It's easy to make and very
forgiving. Fold dough edges over the pears.
The more casual you make it the
more lovely it looks!

An Autumn twist of a dessert classic that is our family's most popular request every Thanksgiving. Pass the blow torch!

Pumpkin Crème Brûlée

Custard:

Preheat oven to 325°F.

2 cups heavy cream

1 vanilla bean or 2 teaspoons vanilla extract

Heat in large glass measuring cup in microwave, 3 minutes. Remove vanilla bean and, with sharp knife, cut open and remove seeds by scraping with knife. Add vanilla seeds to cream.

8 egg yolks

1 cup canned pumpkin

⅓ cup brown sugar

⅓ cup sugar

1 tablespoon pumpkin spice*

½ teaspoon salt

Beat in large bowl.
Add little bit of heated cream mixture while whisking egg yolks. Keep whisking and add egg mixture back to heated cream mixture. (NOTE: This tempers the eggs and prevents them from scrambling.)

Pour mixture into 10-inch tart ceramic baking dish or pie plate. (Small ramekins will work, as well.) Place in WATER BATH** and bake, 40 to 45 minutes or until mixture is set.

Glaze:

Cool and chill at least 1 hour.

¼ cup sugar

Spread ¼ cup sugar evenly over top of custard. Shake pie plate gently to create even layer of sugar. Heat with blow torch or under broiler, 1 to 2 minutes, until golden brown. Garnish, if desired, with fresh whipped cream.

TIPS:

*Can substitute pumpkin spice with 1 teaspoon cinnamon, ½ teaspoon nutmeg, ½ teaspoon ginger and ¼ teaspoon allspice.

**WATER BATH: Place filled tart baking dish in rimmed baking pan that will fit the tart baking dish (half sheet pan works well). Carefully fill 1-inch high with water. This helps the crème brûlée bake evenly and not overcook. Allow hot water to cool before removing the tart baking dish. Carefully remove tart baking dish from water bath.

Crème brûlée mixture can be made three days ahead. Just add glaze and blow torch before serving.

*Makes
16 Servings*

Christmas Eve

Feast Of The Seven Fishes

Jumbo Shrimp Cocktail *with* Red and Green Dipping Sauces

Baked Clams Oreganata

Grandma's Stuffed Vinegar Peppers

Broccoli *with* Garlic and Oil

Marinated Cauliflower Jardiniere

Baccalà Salad *with* Lemon and Parsley

Linguini *with* White Clam Sauce

Garlic Roasted Shrimp Scampi

Broiled Lobster Tails *with* Herbed Butter

Stuffed Calamari over Linguini

Tiramisu Alia

Zeppole

Creamy Cannoli *with* Mini Chocolate Chips

Struffoli

Give your shrimp cocktail a boost with this herb and lemon infusion. Serve with these festive sauces. My late father-in-law would make his own colorful crushed ice by using red and green food coloring in ice cube trays and crushing it up himself. I was so impressed!

Jumbo Shrimp Cocktail *with* Red and Green Dipping Sauces

Makes 6 to 8 Servings

4 quarts water

2 lemons, cut in half

½ bunch Italian parsley stems (with leaves)

5 to 6 chive stems

3 to 4 thyme stems (lemon thyme, if available)

1 teaspoon salt

⅛ teaspoon pepper

Add to large stock pot. Bring to a boil and simmer 3 minutes.

2 pounds colossal or jumbo shrimp (8/12 count for colossal and 16/20 count for jumbo), shelled and deveined (keep tails on)

Add to stock pot. Bring to a boil and cook 2 to 3 minutes or until pink. DO NOT OVERCOOK.

Remove shrimp with a slotted spoon. Plunge immediately in ice water bowl to stop cooking process. (This is called blanching which "shock", the shrimp from overcooking.) Cool and drain. Place in large bowl. Chill.

Red Cocktail Sauce:

1 bottle (14 ounces) cocktail sauce, about 1½ cups

2 tablespoons horseradish

2 to 3 chive stems, snipped, about 1 tablespoon

1 lemon, zested and juiced

Salt and pepper

Combine in small bowl. Chill.

Green Cocktail Sauce:

2 bunches watercress

½ cup sour cream or plain Greek yogurt

2 tablespoons mayonnaise

½ lemon, juiced

Salt and pepper

Blend in food processor until smooth. Chill. Serve sauces with shrimp.

TIP:

Serve shrimp well chilled in cocktail dishes with two small ramekins, one with red cocktail sauce and the other with green cocktail sauce, for beautiful presentation. Garnish with lemon wedges.

135

Baked Clams Oreganata

Preheat oven to 450°F.

2 dozen steamer clams, 2 to 2½ inches wide (try and get the larger sized ones), scrubbed

1 cup dry white wine or water

Place clams in single layer on rimmed baking sheet. Pour white wine or water on top and cover with aluminum foil tightly. Bake 15 to 20 minutes or until clams open or place in large stock pot with 1-inch deep water and boil, covered, 2 to 5 minutes or until shells open. Discard any unopened or broken shells.

Pull clam shells apart so they are two separate halves and remove clam meat. Chop clams and set aside. Place clam shells on two baking sheets.

2 tablespoons extra virgin olive oil

2 tablespoons butter

⅛ teaspoon crushed red pepper flakes

4 cloves garlic, finely chopped

1 large shallot, chopped

Cook in large skillet on medium heat about 5 minutes or until fragrant.

4 ounces pancetta, chopped

Add to skillet. Cook until crisp.

¼ cup dry white wine (your favorite)

Add to skillet and cook until almost all liquid evaporates.

3 tablespoons fresh oregano leaves, finely chopped*

1 large bunch Italian parsley, finely chopped

3 cups fresh breadcrumbs (Italian or Semolina bread, coarsely processed in food processor)**

2 cans (6.5 ounces each) minced clams, drained, reserve juice

½ cup grated Pecorino Romano cheese

¼ cup grated Parmesan cheese

2 to 3 tablespoons extra virgin olive oil

½ to ¾ cup reserved clam juice

Salt and pepper

Combine in large bowl until mixture is moist and holds together slightly.

Fill each clam shell with breadcrumb mixture pressing down firmly. Secure edges.

2 tablespoons extra virgin olive oil

Hungarian paprika (optional)

}

Drizzle clam shells lightly.
Sprinkle with paprika, if desired.

Bake, 5 to 6 minutes or until heated through
and breadcrumbs are browned and crispy.
Garnish, if desired, wtih extra parsley
leaves and lemon wedges.

TIPS:

Substitute oregano leaves with
2 teaspoons dried oregano.

**Can substitute with Panko or plain dried*
breadcrumbs.

Clam recipe can be made one day ahead or
frozen up to three weeks. Broil just before
serving, 2 to 3 minutes, or until heated through.

For extra crunch: Top prepared stuffed
shells with ½ cup panko breadcrumbs,
1 tablespoon grated Parmesan or Pecorino
Romano cheese, 2 teaspoons dried oregano
and drizzle with extra virgin olive oil.

Recipe can easily be doubled (they go fast).

Makes 48 Clams
on the Half Shell

This dish will
be the first to be
wiped clean.

Grandma's Stuffed Vinegar Peppers

2 cups fresh breadcrumbs
(Italian or Semolina bread, processed in food processer until fine)*

Preheat oven to 400°F.

Bake, about 3 to 5 minutes or until lightly toasted on baking sheet. Set aside

½ cup raisins or currants
½ cup pignoli (pine nuts), toasted
½ cup walnuts, coarsely chopped
Salt and pepper

Combine in large bowl with breadcrumbs.

½ gallon mellow red wine (light Chianti), Grandma preferred (Carlo Rossi Paisano®)
1 cup sugar

Bring to a boil in large pot. Cook, 2 hours or until liquid is reduced by half and reaches a slight syrupy consistency.

2 jars (32 ounces each) sweet or vinegar peppers**, combination of red and green, drained and seeded (about 24 to 30 peppers)
1 can (6 ounces) pitted small black olives, drained (about 24 to 30 olives)***

Stuff peppers with breadcrumb mixture. Place one olive in center of each pepper. Set aside.

4 tablespoons extra virgin olive oil

Heat in large skillet. Add stuffed peppers browning bottoms, about 2 minutes.

Pour reduced wine into large skillet, about 1-inch deep. Simmer, covered, basting occasionally, 10 to 15 minutes or until peppers are tender.

Place in plastic container. Cover with remaining reduced wine. Chill up to one week ahead.

Serve at room temperature.

TIPS:

*Can substitute with Panko or plain dried breadcrumbs.

**I like to use the smaller peppers because they are more tender and a great addition to your holiday antipasto.

***You'll only use about three-quarters of 6 ounce can of olives. Save remaining for a salad or another use.

Makes
16 Servings

My mother-in-law Elisa, taught me
this recipe the first year my husband and
I were married. We would joke that the fumes from the
wine got us a little tipsy and we laughed and giggled
the whole time we stuffed these delicious peppers. It is
one of my most precious memory of her. They are the
perfect combination of sweet and sour,
and treasured by our whole family.

Broccoli *with* Garlic and Oil

4 cloves garlic, finely sliced

½ cup extra virgin olive oil

Add to 2-cup heatproof glass measuring cup. Microwave, 1 minute (or heat mixture in small saucepan over low heat, 3 minutes or until garlic is lightly golden). This will make garlic sweeter, removing bitterness and infusing olive oil. Set aside.

2 heads broccoli, trimmed and cut into 2-inch pieces

1 teaspoon salt

Heat large pot with water. Bring to a boil.

Add broccoli.

Cook, 5 minutes until tender, 10 minutes if prefer it softer or 15 minutes if prefer a soupier consistency. Drain. Add to olive oil mixture. Salt and pepper to taste.

Makes 8 to 10 Servings

TIP:

Add grated Parmesan, Pecorino Romano cheese or crushed red pepper flakes for extra seasoning.

This dish was my Dad's favorite. So simple, yet so healthy and hearty. Because he grew up during the Great Depression, he would lick his plate clean every time! My dad would say "Alyssa, you just have that magic touch."

Marinated Cauliflower Jardiniere

Fill large bowl with ice and water.
Bring large saucepan filled with water to a boil. Add 1 teaspoon salt.

1 large head cauliflower,
cut into small florets

4 carrots, peeled and sliced
into ½-inch diagonal slices

Add to boiling water. Cook 3 minutes or until tender.
Remove vegetables with a slotted spoon. Plunge immediately in ice water bowl to stop cooking process. (This is called blanching which "shock", the vegetables from overcooking.) Cool and drain. Place in large bowl.

1 red pepper, seeded and
cut into 1-inch pieces

1 cup Kalamata or Niçoise olives, pitted
and halved (or any black cured olives)

2 lemons, zested and juiced

¼ cup white wine vinegar or
white balsamic vinegar

1 bunch Italian parsley, chopped

¼ teaspoon hot red pepper flakes

3 to 4 anchovy filets (optional),
roughly chopped

Salt and pepper

Add to cauliflower mixture. Toss well.
Chill, 2 hours or overnight

TIP:

Can be made up to two days ahead to marry flavors.

Recipe can be easily doubled.

Makes
8 Servings

This has an
acidic bite but as it marinates it
gets better and better. Great to pair
with assorted Italian cured meats
and cheeses.

I can remember my grandmother
setting an alarm to change the water!
But don't worry overnight! All the
work is in the soaking when you are
sleeping, but so worth the effort.

Baccalà Salad *with* Lemon and Parsley

2 pounds dried and salted cod (baccalà) cut into 3 to 4-inch pieces

Cover with cool water in large bowl. Refrigerate, 2 to 3 days, changing water every 3 to 4 hours, (but don't worry about it when you're sleeping). This rehydrates dried fish and also removes the salt.

½ cup white wine (your favorite)

1 lemon, halved

2 bay leaves

Add to stock pot filled with 6 quarts of water. Bring to a boil. Add soaked cod. Simmer, 5 minutes or until fish is tender and falls apart easily. Strain. Cool. Remove any bones or skin. Break into bite size pieces in large bowl.

⅓ cup extra virgin olive oil

4 to 5 cloves garlic, thinly sliced

Cook on medium high heat about 5 minutes, until golden.

1 lemon, zested and juiced, to taste

1 tablespoon red wine vinegar, to taste

1 cup Kalamata or Niçoise olives, pitted and halved (or any black cured olives)

2 stalks celery, thinly sliced

1 red onion, thinly sliced

1 Fresno chili pepper (for added spice) or red bell pepper, chopped

2 tablespoons capers, drained

1 bunch Italian parsley, chopped

Freshly ground pepper

Combine in large bowl with garlic and olive oil mixture and prepared cod. Chill until serving.

Makes about 4 Cups Salad

TIPS:

Can rehydrate cod up to one week ahead.

Can dress cod up to one day ahead.

Linguini *with* White Clam Sauce

½ cup extra virgin olive oil

6 to 8 cloves garlic, finely chopped

½ teaspoon red pepper flakes

In a large skillet, heat olive oil on medium high heat. Add and cook until garlic is fragrant, about 2 to 3 minutes.

¼ cup white wine (your favorite)

Add wine. Let evaporate, 2 to 3 minutes.

1 bottle (6 ounces) bottled clam juice

1 bunch parsley, chopped

Salt and pepper

Add to skillet. Heat through. Clam sauce mixture can be made up to two hours ahead.

1 can (12 ounces) chopped clams with juice

1 can (12 ounces) clams with juice

3 dozen fresh littleneck clams, cleaned and scrubbed*

Add while pasta cooks. Cover. Bring to a boil and cook 5 minutes or until clam shells open. Discard all unopened clams.

1 pound linguini

Cook pasta according to package directions. Drain pasta, reserving ½ cup pasta water. Toss pasta with clam mixture and reserved pasta water. Garnish, if desired, with whole clams and sprinkle with additional parsley.

TIPS:

*Can substitute littleneck clams with little cockle clams if available - so tiny but so sweet and they have a bluish green shell.

Add 1 cup cherry tomatoes the same time you add the clam shells. Garnish, if desired, with fresh basil leaves.

Add chopped raw bacon or pancetta when cooking the garlic until slightly crisp and proceed as above.

Perfect with toasted Italian bread drizzled with extra virgin olive oil and freshly grated Pecorino Romano or Parmesan cheese.

Makes about 4 to 6 Servings

My daughter Marisa'a says,
"Linguini with White Clam Sauce is
my ultimate favorite of my Mom's
dishes and my most requested,
no matter the occasion."

Just a classic!

Garlic Roasted Shrimp Scampi

Preheat oven to 450°F.

1 cup (2 sticks) butter, melted
¼ cup extra virgin olive oil
1 tablespoon Dijon mustard
4 to 5 cloves garlic, chopped
¼ cup dry white wine (your favorite)

Combine in large shallow baking dish or roasting pan.

2 pounds large shrimp
(26/30 count per pound) peeled and
deveined, with tails on
(if desired, looks prettier)

Toss with butter mixture. Bake, 10 to 15 minutes, or until shrimp turns pink, stirring occasionally.

1 lemon, zested and juiced
1 bunch Italian parsley stems removed,
chopped

Toss and serve.

TIP:

Delicious over linguini or spaghetti. Toss with pasta. Add a little reserved pasta water to combine easily. Also terrific over your favorite rice.

Makes 8 to 10 Servings

The most anticipated
seventh fish of the magical night
of Christmas Eve. My oldest daughter
Maria would say, "When Mom would
start to prepare the lobster, we new
the best was yet to come,"

Broiled Lobster Tails *with* Herbed Butter

Preheat oven to broil.

8 large lobster tails
(about 4 to 6 ounces each)

Cut or snip curved side of shell (backside) vertically with kitchen shears or sharp knife, about ½-inch deep into lobster meat. Pry open sides of shell to detach most of lobster meat, exposing and lifting it slightly. Open the lobster meat with sharp knife to butterfly it. Be careful not to tear or separate the lobster meat. (Lobster meat will now sit on top of the shell with tail tucked in to secure.)

5 to 6 cloves garlic, chopped

1 cup (2 sticks) butter

Melt together in medium saucepan or microwave in heatproof glass measuring cup, 1 minute.

2 lemons, zested and juiced

¼ cup chives, snipped

½ cup Italian parsley with stems removed, chopped

Salt and pepper

Add to butter mixture.
Reserve half of mixture and set aside.
Place lobster tails on shallow baking pan.

Brush half of the butter mixture onto lobster meat.

Broil 12 to 15 minutes or until lobster is pink and opaque.

Serve with remaining herbed butter sauce.

*Makes
8 Servings*

TIPS:

Make sure lobster shells are pried open well so lobster meat cooks and puffs for gorgeous presentation.

Garnish, if desired, with extra lemon wedges, chives and parsley.

Prepare the lobster the morning of dinner and then just broil before serving.

Recipe can be easily doubled.

Stuffed Calamari Over Linguini

12 (4 to 5-inch) whole squid (calamari)

Remove inside cartilage and discard. Remove tentacles and fins. Slice 2 tubes into ¼-inch rings. Reserve. Set aside remaining 10 tubes.

¼ cup extra virgin olive oil

2 cloves garlic, finely chopped

¼ teaspoon hot red pepper flakes

1 teaspoon anchovy paste, (optional)*

Heat olive oil, 1 minute, in large skillet on medium heat. Add remaining ingredients. Cook, about 2 to 3 minutes or until fragrant. Stir until melted if using anchovy paste.

2 to 3 tablespoons dry white wine (your favorite)

Add and cook until almost evaporated.

1 cup fresh fresh breadcrumbs (Italian or Semolina bread, processed in food processer until fine)**

Add and toast until golden. Place mixture in medium bowl.

8 ounces cooked crabmeat

2 eggs, slightly beaten

1 bunch Italian parsley, chopped (about 1 cup)

Salt and pepper

Add to bowl. Stir until combined. Fill 10 squid tubes ¾'s full with stuffing mixture. Crisscross tops with toothpicks to close. (Tradition is to sew them with thread. I use unflavored dental floss, but up to you!)

Makes 6 to 8 Servings

3 tablespoons butter

2 tablespoons extra virgin olive oil

Add to large skillet. Heat, 1 minute over low heat. Add stuffed tubes. Cook over medium heat, 3 minutes or until lightly browned. Add reserved sliced tubes with reserved tentacles and fins. Cook over medium high heat, about 2 more minutes.

¼ cup dry white wine (your favorite)

½ teaspoon hot red pepper flakes (If desired for extra heat kick!)

Add to skillet. Cook until almost evaporated.

4 cups Marinara Sauce (see page 50)

Add to skillet. Cook over medium low heat, 40 minutes, stirring occasionally, or until calamari is very tender when poked with fork.

1 pound linguini or thin spaghetti

Cook according to package directions.

Reserve ½ cup pasta water to thin out marinara sauce if becomes too thick. Remove toothpicks. Slice calamari into ½ to 1-inch pieces. Serve with linguini, sauce and extra hot cracked pepper seeds.

TIPS:

*Anchovy paste gives awesome flavor boost.

**Can substitute Panko or plain dried breadcrumbs.

Tubes can be stuffed one day ahead.

One of my husband's favorites! It's traditionally served on Christmas Eve with my in-laws. I added my own twist with fresh crabmeat. It's a little work but worth it if you're a seafood lover.

Tiramisu "Alia" Style

6 large egg yolks

1 cup confectioner's sugar

Whisk together in heatproof bowl set over pot of simmering water or double boiler, 5 to 10 minutes, stirring constantly so eggs don't scramble, until slightly thickened or temperature reaches 160°F with instant-read thermometer. Place in large bowl of an electric mixer and beat, about 5 to 10 minutes or until thick.

Makes about 12 Servings

8 ounces mascarpone

Add and beat until smooth.

2 cups heavy cream

In chilled large bowl of an electric mixer, beat on high speed until cream starts to thicken about 2 to 3 minutes.

½ cup confectioner's sugar

1 teaspoon vanilla

Slowly add and continue to beat until soft peaks form, about 3 to 5 minutes. Reserve 1 cup whipped cream. Set aside for garnish. Fold remaining whipped cream into mascarpone mixture. Set aside.

¼ cup hot water

1 tablespoon instant espresso

1 tablespoon rum*

3 tablespoons sugar

Mix in glass measuring cup or small bowl.

2 packages (3 ounce each) 48 ladyfingers

Brush ladyfingers with rum mixture. Arrange in single layer in a 9 x 13-inch glass baking dish or 9 x 9-inch deep dish baking dish. Do not soak cookies or will become too moist. Spread half mascarpone cream evenly with spatula on top of brushed ladyfingers. Repeat with second layer of brushed ladyfingers and remaining mascarpone cream. Chill, at least 2 hours or overnight.

Unsweetened cocoa powder

Chocolate shavings/chocolate curls

Garnish with reserved whipped cream. Use large star tip with pastry bag for piping for pretty topping. Sprinkle cocoa powder and chocolate curls on top.

TIPS:

*Can substitute rum with coffee liqueur.

To make chocolate curls: Heat 2 ounces chocolate chunks in microwave, 30 seconds. Use vegetable peeler to scrape chocolate towards you to make curls. (If curls break, place chocolate back in microwave at 30 second intervals until desired softness.) Do not touch with hands. They're delicate and may break. Pick up with toothpick and carefully place onto tiramisu to "wow" guests.

Can assemble in 9-inch springform pan. Line bottom with parchment paper. Use additional 3 ounce package ladyfingers and increase rum by half, placing ladyfingers straight up alongside springform pan as you layer.

Can be made up to two days ahead.

154

Tiramisu has become a popular dessert on many Italian restaurant menus. It's the perfect end to any special meal.

Zeppole

| Canola or vegetable oil | } | *In a deep fryer, fill with oil. Preheat to 375°F.* |

2 cups all-purpose flour		
½ cup sugar	}	*Combine in large bowl.*
1 tablespoon baking powder		
1 teaspoon salt		

3 eggs, lightly beaten		
2 pounds whole milk ricotta	}	*Combine. Add to flour mixture.*
1 tablespoon vanilla extract		

Spoon rounded tablespoon batter (or use 1½-inch ice cream scoop) into hot oil. Fry, 3 to 5 minutes, or until golden and puffed. Drain on paper towel-lined baking sheet.

| Confectioner's sugar | } | *Sprinkle immediately. Serve hot!* |

Makes about 3 Dozen

TIP:
Can make zeppole up to 2 hours ahead. Reheat in oven 350°F, 5 to 10 minutes or until warm to the touch.

Christmas Eve was always my favorite holiday as a child. I remember sitting under the serving table laden with Italian cookies and sweets while watching the dancing feet of my aunts, uncles and cousins. After the Feast of the Seven Fishes and midnight mass, we would continue the festivities in our basement with my grandfather's player piano while everyone sang and danced. My godfather would be in the basement kitchen making pizza and frying zeppoli. It was an all night party filled with loving memories! En-Joy!

One of my favorite memories is rolling out cannoli dough
for the shells with my Dad. It takes some muscle power to do it by hand,
but they can be rolled out in a pasta machine, too. As an alternative, make
the cream and buy the shells at your local Italian bakery.
This filling is light and can be served alone in a dessert cup
with chopped cannoli shells on top, as well.

Creamy Cannoli *with* Mini Chocolate Chips

Cannoli Shells:

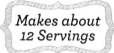

Makes about
12 Servings

3 cups all-purpose flour
1 teaspoon baking powder
¼ cup sugar
1 teaspoon cinnamon
1 teaspoon salt

Combine in large bowl.

2 tablespoons unsalted butter
2 tablespoons shortening

Cut into flour mixture with two knives or pastry blender until resembles coarse crumbs.

2 eggs, beaten
2 tablespoons white wine for light shells or red wine for darker shells (your choice)

Add and mix lightly until binds and forms ball. Wrap in plastic wrap. Chill for at least 30 minutes. Divide dough into four pieces and roll out each piece to ⅛-inch thick. Cut using 4½-inch circle cookie cutter.

Canola oil

In a deep fryer, fill with oil. Preheat to 375°F.

1 egg white

Wrap dough around cannoli forms*. Overlap edges and seal by brushing with egg white for glue. Press edges to seal well. Fry, 2 to 3 minutes or until golden brown. Let cool slightly before removing forms.

Cannoli Filling:

1 container (15 ounces) whole milk ricotta**

Drain, 24 hours in fine strainer lined with paper towels or cheesecloth. Straining ricotta removes water so cannoli cream is thick.

¾ cup heavy cream

In chilled large bowl of an electric mixer, beat on high speed until cream starts to thicken, about 2 to 3 minutes.

1 cup confectioner's sugar
1 tablespoon vanilla extract

Slowly add and continue to beat until soft peaks form, about 3 to 4 minutes. Gently fold whipped cream into strained ricotta.

½ cup mini chocolate chips

Fill cannoli shells using pastry bag with large ½-inch star tip. Fill immediately before serving so shells do not get soggy. Sprinkle filled ends with chips. Sprinkle, if desired additional with confectioner's sugar.

TIPS:

*Cannoli forms give cannoli shells their iconic shape. Purchase online or at a speciality cookware store.

**Substitute whole milk ricotta with ricotta impastata found in speciality Italian or restaurant supply stores. Use 1 cup heavy cream, whipped, in this filling.

For extra special look, dip cannoli shells in melted semi-sweet chocolate.

Cannoli shells can be made up to one month ahead and stored in airtight container.

Struffoli

Canola or vegetable oil	In a deep fryer, fill with oil. Preheat to 375°F.
3 cups all-purpose flour 1 tablespoon sugar 2 teaspoons baking powder ½ teaspoon salt	Combine in medium bowl.

Makes about 20 Cups Struffoli, about 6 Small Wreaths

6 eggs	Make a well in center of flour and add eggs into middle of well. Slowly mix flour from edges into eggs until combined, using fork. Knead on floured surface, 5 to 10 minutes or until dough is as smooth as a baby's behind (my Nana would say). Dough should bounce back when pressed with your finger. Turn onto floured bowl and cover with plastic wrap. Let rest, 30 to 45 minutes.

*Cut small piece of dough on floured cutting board. Roll into ½-inch wide rope. Cut into ½-inch pieces. Let pieces stand at least 30 minutes before frying to dry out a little. Dust with additional flour. This will prevent them from sticking together. Place struffoli in fine strainer, in batches and shake off excess flour before frying. Fry until golden. Let rest on paper towels to drain.

Our new addition to the Struffoli team!

1 pound honey	Heat in medium sauce pan to hard crack stage (350°F) on candy thermometer. Toss struffoli immediately in large bowl with honey.
Nonpareil sprinkles, multicolored or holiday colors	Turn struffoli immediately onto parchment paper lined board. Form into wreath shapes with wet hands. Top immediately with sprinkles.

TIPS:

*Short Cut: dough can be flattened slightly on well floured board. With rolling pin, roll to ¼-inch thick, using extra flour so rolling pin does not stick. Cut horizontally into ½-inch wide strips. Then cut each strip into ½-inch squares and let dry as above, 30 minutes. When they fry they will puff into ball shapes.

Keep Struffoli Wreaths in air tight container up to one week. This recipe is definitely a team effort. Get your whole family involved and have fun!

160

This recipe is probably the most sentimental for me. Struffoli, also known as honey balls, always bring the family together in the preparation. I learned how to make them at an early age from my Nana. Then, I made them every year with my Mom. I was the cutter and she was the fryer. Now my girls cut and I fry. It's a time consuming job that can be quickly accomplished with help. Our version of traditional Italian struffoli is heartwarming. Dunk the leftover struffoli in your coffee on Christmas morning while opening presents with family.

Christmas

Christmas Day

Antipasti Selection
Eggplant Stacks with Fresh Mozzarella and Balsamic Glaze
Marinated Stuffed Olives • *Prosciutto with Melon*

Sugar & Spice Glazed Holiday Pecans

Grilled Polenta *with* Festive Olive Tapenade and Gorgonzola

Lasagna Bolognese *with* Mini Meatballs

Herbed Beef Tenderloin Roast Wrapped *with*
Bacon, Red Onion Relish and Horseradish Cream

Nana's Stuffed Artichokes

Stuffed Mushrooms *with* Sausage and Herbs

Green Beans *with* Toasted Almonds

Crème Brûlée *with* Raspberries

Creamy Risotto Rice Pudding

Holiday Ice Cream Mud Pie

Cannoli Cheesecake

Candy Cane Fudgie Brownies

Peppermint Bark

Peanut Butter Chocolate Kiss Cookies

Toffee Bars

Walnut Snowballs

Citrus Biscotti

Nana's Almond Crescents

Linzer Bar Triangles

Pignoli Cookies

Love Knots *with* Red and Green Nonpareils

Eggplant Stacks *with* Fresh Mozzarella and Balsamic Glaze

Preheat oven to 400°F.
Lay out 3 shallow dinner size plates or large paper plates.

2 tablespoons extra virgin olive oil } *Brush on shallow baking sheet lightly and set aside.*

½ teaspoon salt
¼ teaspoon ground pepper
½ cup all-purpose flour } *Combine in first plate.*

4 large eggs, beaten
1 lemon, juiced } *Combine in second plate.*

1½ cups fresh breadcrumbs
(Italian or Semolina bread, processed in
food processer until fine)*
1 bunch Italian parsley, coarsely chopped
⅓ cup grated Parmesan cheese } *Combine in third plate.*

1 medium eggplant, sliced into 12 to 14
rounds crosswise, about ⅛-inch thick } *Dip eggplant in flour, egg mixture and then breadcrumb mixture to completely coat.*

Place eggplant slices in single layer on parchment-lined baking sheet. Drizzle with additional 1 tablespoon olive oil to lightly coat. Bake, 15 to 20 minutes or until golden brown and crisp.

12 ounces fresh mozzarella, ovoline size,
sliced into 6 to 7 slices each } *Place on 1 slice of eggplant. Top with second slice of eggplant to make sandwich stack.*

Bake 10 minutes or until cheese is melted and heated through.

¼ cup balsamic glaze**
Basil leaves } *Drizzle over eggplant sandwiches. Garnish with basil leaves. Serve warm or at room temperature.*

TIPS:

*Can substitute with Panko or plain dried breadcrumbs.

**Substitute balsamic glaze with marinara sauce (see page 48).

Eggplant can be baked and frozen up to one month ahead.

Great for last minute sandwiches or a quick dinner.

Makes about 8 Servings

These little stacks
are just delightful as
an appetizer
or main dish.

Stuffing the olives is a perfect job for any little one. My daughter Marisa started to help me in the kitchen at three years old with this recipe. You may want to double it because they'll be eaten as you're making them.

Marinated Stuffed Olives

1 chunk (8 ounces) provolone, sliced into small sticks, about 1⅛-inch

2 cans (13 ounces each) colossal pitted black olives, drained

} *Insert provolone into olive cavities.*

¼ cup extra virgin olive oil

2 cloves garlic, finely chopped

Salt and pepper

} *Add to 2-cup heatproof glass measuring cup. Microwave for 1 minute (or heat mixture in small saucepan over low heat, 3 minutes.) This will make garlic sweeter, removing bitterness and infusing olive oil with flavor.) Set aside.*

1 red pepper, finely chopped

1 yellow pepper, finely chopped

½ cup Italian parsley, chopped

½ teaspoon crushed red pepper flakes

} *Combine in small bowl with infused olive oil. Toss with olives.*

Makes about 60 to 70 Olives

TIPS:

Can be easily halved or doubled.

Can be made one day ahead.

Prosciutto *with* Melon

16 very thin slices of prosciutto
(about 6 ounces)

1 large cantaloupe and/or honeydew melon,
sliced into 16 wedges

Wrap prosciutto around melon

1 lemon, halved

*Squeeze lemon on prepared melon
before serving. Serve, if desired,
with lemon wedges.*

*Makes sbout
8 Servings*

TIP:

*Can wrap the melon four hours before
serving. Place on platter, wrap with plastic
wrap and chill.*

*So classic and simple.
This was a special first course
for almost every holiday!*

I make these on the fly
for so many occasions. They are
perfect to serve with cocktails
when your company arrives.

Sugar & Spice Glazed Holiday Pecans

1 pound pecan halves* (about 6 cups)

1 egg white

½ cup sugar

¼ cup butter, melted

1 teaspoon cinnamon or pumpkin spice

½ teaspoon sea salt

¼ teaspoon hot red pepper flakes (optional)

Makes about 6 Cups

Preheat oven to 350°F.

Combine on parchment lined baking sheet.

Bake, 10 to 15 minutes, stirring occasionally, or until browned and sugar is melted.

TIPS:

*Can substitute using your favorite nut.

Can be stored in air-tight container up to one month ahead.

Replace cinnamon with cumin and add 1½ teaspoons chili powder, add ¼ teaspoon oregano, for a savory option.

Makes a wonderful holiday and hostess gift, too!

Grilled Polenta *with*
Festive Olive Tapenade and Gorgonzola

3 cups chicken broth or water } *Bring to a boil in a large saucepan.*

1 cup polenta or cornmeal
1 teaspoon salt } *Sprinkle into saucepan slowly. Stir constantly, about 10 to 15 minutes or until thickened.*

½ cup grated Parmesan cheese
1 tablespoon butter } *Stir into polenta. Immediately pour mixture onto lightly olive oiled 9 x 13-inch baking pan. Chill until firm. Cut into 12 squares, then 24 triangles.*

2 tablespoons butter } *Add to large skillet or grill pan and cook over medium high heat until melted. Add polenta triangles, turning once and cook until golden. Set aside.*

2 cloves garlic, finely chopped
½ bunch fresh Italian parsley, chopped
2 to 3 sprigs fresh thyme
(or 1 teaspoon dried) } *Add to food processor and process until finely chopped.*

½ cup pitted Kalamata olives
½ cup green olives, pitted
(Castelvetrano are my favorite!)
½ cup sun-dried tomatoes in oil, drained } *Add to food processor and roughly chop (pulse once or twice).*

1 tablespoon extra virgin olive oil
1 lemon, zested } *Stir in.*

8 ounces gorgonzola or Danish bleu cheese,
sliced or crumbled } *Top polenta triangles with 1 heaping teaspoon olive tapenade and cheese.*

TIPS:

Tapenade and polenta triangles can be made one day ahead.

If desired, after chilled, brush with butter and broil until golden. Let cool and cut into squares or triangles and proceed as above.

Makes 24 Appetizers

One of my favorite food memories is of my Nana making polenta for our family. I have loved it ever since.

This dish is always served as a course itself and the one my family craves the most every Christmas. The mini meatballs in the lasagna were a tradition growing up in my household and I loved making them with my Nana as a child. Now my girls love making them with me!

Lasagna Bolognese with Mini Meatballs

Mini Meatballs:*

2 pounds meatloaf mixture (ground veal, pork and beef)

½ Italian bread loaf (preferably 1 or 2 days old), soaked in ½ cup water until soft

¼ cup grated Parmesan cheese

¼ cup grated Pecorino Romano cheese

3 eggs

1 teaspoon salt

¼ teaspoon ground pepper

1 bunch Italian parsley, chopped, about 1 cup

Preheat oven to 350°F.

Combine in large bowl and mix well.

Roll mixture into ½-inch meatballs*. (Makes about 180 to 200 mini meatballs. depending upon who is doing the rolling.)

Place rolled meatballs on parchment-lined rimmed baking sheet drizzled with olive oil. (half sheet pan works great)

Bake, 15 to 20 minutes, turning once, until internal temperature reaches 160°F.

Makes about 180-200 Mini Meatballs

TIPS:

*TIME SAVER: Instead of rolling each meatball individually, brown meatball mixture in large skillet by breaking it up into small pieces. Cook through.

Leftover meatballs can be frozen up to one month.

Continued on page 176

Lasagna Bolognese *with* Mini Meatballs

Lasagna:

Preheat oven to 350°F.

1 container (32 ounces) whole milk ricotta cheese

¾ cup grated Parmesan cheese

¾ cup grated Pecorino Romano cheese

1 bunch Italian parsley, chopped, about 1 cup

1 bunch fresh basil, chopped, about 1 cup

Salt and pepper

Mix in medium bowl. Set aside.

5 cups Marinara Sauce* (See page 48)

9 lasagna noodles, cooked**

1 pound fresh mozzarella*** (preferably water-packed), sliced

2 pounds mini meatballs (See page 175)

1 tablespoon each of grated Parmesan and Pecorino Romano cheese

Spread ½ cup sauce in 9 x 13-inch casserole. Top with three noodles, 1 cup Marinara Sauce, half of ricotta mixture, half of mozzarella and half of mini meatballs. Repeat layers.

Top with remaining 3 lasagna noodles, ½ cup remaining Marinara Sauce and Parmesan and Pecorino Romano cheeses.

Cover with aluminum foil. Bake, 30 to 40 minutes.

Remove aluminum foil. Bake additional 15 minutes or until browned and bubbly. Let stand 30 minutes before serving. Serve with remaining 2 cups Marinara Sauce, heated.

TIP:

*Can substitute Marinara Sauce for Sunday Gravy recipe in "If the Table Could Talk, A Taste of Celebrations" Cookbook.

**Use uncooked lasagna noodles or fresh sheets for no fuss, but use additional ½ cup Marinara Sauce on noodles for each layer.

***Can substitute fresh mozzarella with whole milk shredded mozzarella.

Can prepare lasagna and freeze ahead up to 3 weeks. Bake frozen lasagna covered, at 325°F for 50 to 60 minutes or until center is hot. Change oven temperature to 350°F. Take cover off and bake, 15 minutes to crisp up edges and proceed as above.

Makes about 12 to 16 Servings

The Red Onion Relish and
Horseradish Cream add extra
zest to this moist and delectable
preparation of the meat.

Herbed Beef Tenderloin Roast Wrapped *with* Bacon, Red Onion Relish and Horseradish Cream

Roast:

2 cups fresh breadcrumbs
(Italian or Semolina bread, processed in
food processor until fine)*

1 bunch Italian parsley, chopped

2 teaspoons fresh thyme

3 sprigs fresh rosemary (4-inches long with
stems removed)

2 teaspoons marjoram

¼ cup grated Parmesan cheese

3 tablespoons extra virgin olive oil

4 cloves garlic, chopped

1 lemon, zested

Salt and pepper

Preheat oven to 375°F.

*Makes about
6 to 8 Servings*

Combine in medium bowl. Set aside.

1½ pounds, trimmed and tied,
whole beef tenderloin**

1 tablespoon extra virgin olive oil

*Season with salt and pepper.
Heat pan on medium high heat.
Add olive oil. Brown tenderloin on all sides,
about 2 to 3 minutes. Place on elevated rack
in roasting pan.*

1 cup Dijon mustard

*Brush with mustard. Top entire filet with
herb mixture.***

*Roast, 35 to 40 minutes or until
an instant-read thermometer reaches
120°F for rare, 125°F for medium rare and
130°F for medium.*

*Allow to rest, 20 minutes before serving.
(This allows all juices to redistribute within
meat and makes it extra juicy.)
Best to slice into ¼-inch slices.*

*Top with Red Onion Relish and
Horseradish Cream (See page 180).*

TIP:

*Can substitute with Panko or plain dried
breadcrumbs.*

**Tenderloin can be prepared and
refrigerated one day ahead up to this point.
Let it come to room temperature
one hour before roasting.*

Red Onion Relish:

½ cup (1 stick) butter
3 large red onions, thinly sliced

Cook over medium heat in large heavy skillet for 1 hour, stirring occasionally, until tender and caramelized.

¼ cup balsamic vinegar

Add to skillet. Continue to cook, 30 minutes or until vinegar has evaporated and mixture is glazed and thick.

½ cup Italian parsley, chopped
Salt and pepper

Add to skillet. Mix together. Serve with roast at room temperature.

Horseradish Cream:

1 pint (16 ounces) sour cream
¼ cup mayonnaise
¼ cup horseradish
2 tablespoons Dijon mustard
2 tablespoons snipped chives
Salt and pepper

Combine in small bowl. Serve with roast.

Makes about 2 cups each

TIP:

Both the Red Onion Relish and Horseradish Cream can be prepared one day ahead.

The meat can also be sliced and served on toasted Italian bread slices as a wonderful appetizer.

Nana's Stuffed Artichokes

2 lemons, halved (prevents browning) } *Fill large stockpot two thirds with water. Add lemons and a bring to a boil.*

12 medium artichokes, leaves trimmed and stems removed (reserve stems) } *Add and cook 10 to 12 minutes (depending on size) or until the leaves pull off easily. Drain and let cool.*

5 cups fresh breadcrumbs (Italian or Semolina bread, processed in food processer until fine)*

1 cup panko breadcrumbs

½ cup grated Parmesan cheese

½ cup grated Pecorino Romano cheese

1 bunch Italian parsley, chopped

½ cup extra virgin olive oil

6 cloves garlic, peeled and finely chopped

Salt and pepper } *Combine. (If too dry, add a little more olive oil. Mixture should hold together slightly.) Fill center and outside leaves of artichokes with breadcrumb mixture. Distribute mixture evenly.*

Preheat oven to 350°F.

2 cups Chicken Stock broth (see page 94), or water

½ cup extra-virgin olive oil

6 cloves garlic, peeled and thinly sliced } *In a large shallow baking pan, add reserved stems, salt and pepper. Place artichokes in prepared pan standing upright. Loosely cover with aluminum foil. Bake, 20 minutes or until tender and heated through.*

Baste occasionally, about every 5 minutes, during cooking time. Remove foil. Broil, 5 minutes or until browned and crispy. Enjoy with juice from roasting pan for dipping.

TIPS:

*Can substitute Panko or plain dried breadcrumbs.

Always use small to medium sizes. If you can only find large artichokes, make sure to blanch them until the leaves pull off easily before you stuff them.

Artichokes can be stuffed one day ahead.

You can also double the chicken stock juice and serve heated with the artichokes for extra dipping.

Makes 12 Artichokes

I videoed my Nana when she was late in her 80's while she showed me how to make these artichokes. I asked "Nana, how do you know how much bread to use?" She replied, "How many people are you having?" I said, "Ten." She began to grab handfuls of bread stuffing, counting to ten. The stuffing filled ten medium artichokes perfectly! It was a useful lesson learned for measuring.

Stuffed Mushrooms *with* Sausage and Herbs

Preheat oven to 400°F.

24 large mushrooms
(about 2-inch diameter), stems removed
(chop stems and reserve)

Place on parchment paper lined baking sheet.

2 tablespoons butter

Melt and brush onto mushroom caps. Set aside.

8 ounces bulk Italian sausage

In a large skillet, cook on medium heat breaking up sausage until browned, about 5 to 10 minutes.

2 cloves garlic, finely chopped
1 small onion, chopped

Add with reserved chopped stems and cook on medium high heat until soft, about 3 to 5 minutes.

2 tablespoons white wine (your favorite)

Add and stir until evaporated.

1 to 1½ cups fresh breadcrumbs
(Italian or Semolina bread, processed in
food processer until fine)*
½ cup grated Pecorino Romano cheese
1 bunch Italian parsley, chopped
(about 1 cup)

Add to skillet just to mix together. Remove from heat. Stuff mushroom caps immediately and evenly.

Extra virgin olive oil
Additional grated Pecorino Romano cheese

Drizzle and sprinkle top of mushrooms.

Bake, 20 to 25 minutes or until mushrooms are tender and lightly browned.

Makes 24 Servings

TIP:

*Can substitute with Panko or plain dried breadcrumbs.

Can make filling one day ahead and stuff mushrooms the day of cooking. Chill. Bake when guests arrive.

Try these savory stuffed mushrooms as a lovely side to your beef tenderloin.

Blanched and sautéed in butter, this adds just the right crunch to your dinner platter.

Green Beans *with* Toasted Almonds

Fill large bowl with ice and water.
Bring large saucepan filled with water to a boil. Add 1 teaspoon salt.

2 pounds green beans, washed and trimmed

Add to boiling water. Cook 4 minutes or until tender.
Remove vegetables with a slotted spoon. Plunge immediately in ice water bowl to stop cooking process. (This is called blanching which "shock", the vegetables from overcooking.) Cool and drain.
Place in large bowl.

4 tablespoons butter

2 cups sliced almonds

Melt butter and add almonds to medium skillet. Cook over medium heat until golden.

Toss with green beans and serve.
Salt and pepper to taste before serving.

Makes about 12 Servings

TIPS:

Beans can be blanched one day ahead and stored in large plastic bag in refrigerator.

Almonds can be toasted one day ahead.

Crème Brûlée *with* Raspberries

Preheat oven to 325°F.

Custard:

3 cups heavy cream

1 vanilla bean or 2 teaspoons vanilla extract

Heat in large glass measuring cup in microwave, 3 minutes.
Remove vanilla bean and, with sharp knife, cut open and remove seeds by scraping with knife. Add vanilla seeds to cream.

6 egg yolks

¾ cup sugar

½ teaspoon salt

Beat in large bowl.
Add little bit of heated cream mixture while whisking egg yolks. Keep whisking and add egg mixture back to heated cream mixture. (NOTE: This tempers the eggs and prevents them from scrambling.)

Pour mixture into 10-inch tart ceramic baking dish or pie plate. (Small ramekins work, as well.) Place in WATER BATH* and bake, 30 to 45 minutes or until mixture is set.

Cool completely and chill at least 1 hour.

Glaze:

¼ cup sugar

Spread ¼ cup sugar evenly over top of custard. Shake pie plate gently to create even layer of sugar. Heat with blow torch or under broiler, about 1 to 2 minutes, until golden brown. Garnish, if desired, with fresh raspberries and mint leaves to resemble a Christmas tree.

TIPS:

*WATER BATH: Place filled tart baking dish in rimmed baking pan that will fit the tart baking dish (half sheet pan works well). Carefully fill 1-inch high with water. This helps the crème brûlée bake evenly and not overcook. When done baking, allow hot water to cool before removing the tart baking dish from water bath.

Crème brûlée mixture can be made three days ahead. Just make glaze and blow torch before serving.

Makes about 16 Servings

Every Christmas,
I gave my daughter Marisa and my cousin Renee
the job of browning the crème brûlée with my
blowtorch. It's always a crowd-pleaser. Then,
Marisa makes a Christmas tree out of raspberries
on top for a festive touch.

This recipe was inspired by my friend Joanne. She is an excellent cook and has always been kind to share recipes and ideas. Here is my adaptation of her Greek family's recipe using risotto instead of regular rice to make this classic an oldie but a goodie!

Creamy Risotto Rice Pudding

2 quarts whole milk

2 vanilla beans or 1 tablespoon vanilla extract

} *Combine in large saucepan. Bring to a boil.*

1¼ cups Arborio rice (regular rice works great, too)

1¼ cups sugar

} *Add to saucepan. Cook on medium low heat, 15 to 20 minutes, stirring occasionally, until rice is almost tender.*

3 eggs plus one egg yolk

} *Beat eggs and yolks in large bowl. Slowly add 1 cup hot rice mixture into egg mixture while whisking constantly. Continue whisking and add egg mixture back into sauce pan with rice mixture (NOTE: This tempers the eggs and prevents them from scrambling.)*

Cook mixture while stirring constantly with wooden spoon on low heat until mixture slightly thickens. Do not overcook or else eggs will scramble. (A good test is to run your finger across back of wooden spoon and if mixture does not run together, it's done, about 10 to 15 minutes.)

Pour into serving bowl.

Cover with plastic wrap directly on rice mixture to prevent skin from forming. Chill, 2 hours.

Cinnamon for garnish } *Sprinkle with cinnamon and serve.*

Makes about 12 Servings

TIPS:

Can be made two days ahead.

Sprinkle cinnamon in diamond pattern then top with fresh whipped cream, for a decorative touch.

My daughters love to make this for the holidays and special occasions. It's like a huge ice cream sundae in a pie. Use any favorite ice cream flavors and toppings. What more can you ask for in a dessert?

Holiday Ice Cream Mud Pie

Preheat oven to 350°F.

1 package (14.3 ounces) chocolate sandwich cookies, reserve 1 for garnish

Crush remaining cookies finely in food processor, about 3½ cups crumbs.

⅓ cup butter, melted

Combine in small bowl with cookie crumbs. Press into bottom and sides of 9-inch pie plate. Bake, 8 minutes. Cool.

1 jar (12 ounces) chocolate fudge sauce and/or caramel sauce

2 pints (16 ounces each) ice cream or frozen yogurt of your choice

Pour half of each sauce on bottom of prepared pie shell. Scoop ice cream and make high mounds. Drizzle remaining sauces on top. Freeze, 2 hours or until firm.

1 cup whipped cream (or your favorite whipped topping)

Nuts, sprinkles and/or crushed candy of your choice

Decorate with piped whipped cream, nuts, sprinkles, crushed candies and reserved cookie on top.

Let sit, 10 minutes at room temperature, for easy cutting. Slice and serve.

Makes about 16 Servings

TIPS:

We use mint ice cream and decorate with crushed candy canes for the holidays. Use any of your favorite flavor combinations.

Can be assembled and frozen up to two days ahead.

Cannoli Cheesecake

Preheat oven to 325°F.

Place shallow baking pan in lower rack of oven (half sheet pan works perfectly). Fill with at least 1-inch water. The moisture from the steam helps prevent the cheesecake from cracking.

Open springform pan. Insert the bottom pan upside down and close springform pan.
Line 9-inch springform pan with circle of parchment paper.
This method allows your cheesecake to slide right off onto your serving plate much easier.
Wrap outside of springform with heavy-duty aluminum foil to prevent
any seeping of butter through pan when baking.

Crust:

1 package (10.1 ounces) finely crushed shortbread-type cookies (about 2¾ cups)

2 tablespoons sugar

⅓ cup (5 tablespoons) butter, melted

Combine in bowl.
Press firmly into bottom and slightly up the sides of springform pan.
Bake, 8 minutes. Cool.

Batter:

3 packages (8 ounces each) cream cheese, softened

1½ cups sugar

In large bowl of electric mixer, beat on high speed until light and fluffy, about 5 minutes.

1 container (15 ounces) whole milk ricotta (about 1¾ cups)

Add to bowl. Beat on medium speed until smooth.

3 tablespoons cornstarch
½ cup sour cream
1 teaspoon vanilla extract
1 teaspoon salt

Add to bowl. Beat on low speed until smooth, about 1 minute.

5 eggs

Add one at a time and beat on low speed until blended, about 1 minute. DO NOT OVERBEAT. (This also helps prevent cheesecake from cracking.) Stir in.

1 bag (12 ounces) mini semi-sweet chocolate chips

Pour batter over crust into prepared springform pan. Place on middle rack of oven. Bake, 1 hour and 20 minutes or until center is almost set. Let cool.

Chill 2 hours or overnight.

Makes about 12 to 16 Servings

194

This cheesecake is an unbeatable choice for any special occasion. It's a traditional ricotta cheesecake but is also super creamy.

TIPS:

Pipe with star tip or dollop whipped cream to decorate cheesecake. Garnish with mini cannoli shells filled with whipped cream and mini chocolate chips. Sprinkle with confectioner's sugar.

Can be made three days ahead and/or frozen up to one month ahead.

To make fresh whipped cream: Beat 1 cup heavy cream in chilled bowl of electric mixer on high speed until starts to thicken. Slowly add ¼ cup confectioners sugar. Whip on high speed until thickened and makes soft peaks when beater is lifted.

I love the combination of chocolate and mint! My husband proposed to me on a peppermint pattie. It's my favorite candy! Add this rich, candy cane chocolate brownie to your holiday cookie or dessert tray.

Makes about 4 Dozen Squares

Candy Cane Fudgie Brownies

Preheat oven to 325°F.

Line 12½ x 17½ x 1-inch half sheet baking pan with heavy-duty aluminum foil, extended over edges of pan. Spray with non-stick cooking spray, line with parchment paper and spray again. (Remember BPB: The butter, paper, butter rule in baking.) This prevents brownies from sticking to bottom of pan and create easy removal. Set aside.

2½ cups cups all-purpose flour

1 teaspoon baking soda

1 teaspoon salt

Combine in large bowl and set aside.

1½ cups sugar

2 sticks (1 cup) unsalted butter

3 tablespoons water

Combine in large saucepan. Over medium heat, bring to a boil for 1 minute or until sugar is dissolved. Remove from heat.

24 ounces semi-sweet or bittersweet chocolate squares, chopped or broken in small pieces

Add to butter mixture and stir until chocolote is melted. Let cool slightly.

6 eggs, slightly beaten

1 tablespoon vanilla extract

1 teaspoon peppermint extract

Add eggs to chocolate mixture, one at a time, and stir until smooth. Stir in extracts with flour mixture and stir until smooth.

2 cups coarsely chopped walnuts or pecans (optional)

1 bag (12 ounces) semisweet or bittersweet chocolate chips

Stir into brownie mixture until smooth.

Pour into prepared pan. Bake 30 to 35 minutes. IMPORTANT NOT TO OVERBAKE. Brownies will be moist in center and do not come out clean with toothpick test. Cool. Remove entire baked brownie all at once, by lifting and holding foil edges, for easy cutting.

Top, if desired, with Chocolate Minted Candy Cane Ganache* or dust with confectioner's sugar.

*Chocolate Minted Candy Cane Ganache: In medium saucepan, over medium heat, bring 1 cup heavy cream just to a boil. Remove from heat and stir in 2 cups chopped chocolate until smooth. Add 1 teaspoon peppermint extract. Pour over the brownies and spread evenly making swirls with offset spatula. Top with 3 candy canes, crushed, or ½ cup crushed red and white spiral mint candy. Chill to set. Cut brownies with long, hot, sharp knife straight down with one motion for clean, straight edges.

Makes about 4 Dozen Squares

TIPS:

The quality of the chocolate is key here so choose a rich high cocoa ratio in your chocolate such as 60% or 70% cocoa.

Can be served with or without the ganache topping. If you choose without just dust with confectioner's sugar.

Cut brownies in squares and then triangles for a different look.

These can be baked and frozen up to one month ahead. Defrost at room temperature or in refrigerator and then top with Chocolate Minted Candy Cane Ganache.

Peppermint Bark

1 package (16 ounces) semi-sweet chocolate chips (or favorite semi-sweet chocolate), melted

Line cookie sheet or large baking pan with parchment paper.

Pour onto parchment and spread into thin layer.

Place in refrigerator to harden.

1 teaspoon peppermint extract

1 package (16 ounces) white chocolate chips (or favorite white chocolate), melted

Mix extract into white chocolate. Pour mixture on top of semi-sweet chocolate and spread.

6 to 8 candy canes, crushed*

Sprinkle over chocolate. Cool and break into pieces.

Makes 32 to 36 Pieces

TIPS:

*To crush candy canes: Place in disposable plastic bag with zipper and hit with mallet or rolling pin.

Can be made up to one month ahead and stored in airtight container in refrigerator.

A wonderful hostess gift!

This recipe is a favorite of both of my daughters. They would race to see who could put the kisses on the baked cookies the fastest. Your children will love to help roll the dough in sugar and place the perfect chocolate kiss on the warm baked cookies too!

Peanut Butter Chocolate Kiss Cookies

Preheat oven to 375°F.

Line baking sheets with parchment paper.

64 chocolate kisses } *Unwrap and set aside.*

3½ cups all-purpose flour
2 teaspoons baking soda
½ teaspoon salt
} *Combine in medium bowl and set aside.*

1 cup (2 sticks) butter, softened
1½ cups light brown sugar, firmly packed
½ cup granulated sugar
} *Add to bowl large of electric mixer. Beat on medium high speed until light and creamy, about 5 minutes.*

1 cup regular or crunchy peanut butter
2 eggs
2 teaspoons vanilla extract
} *Add to butter mixture. Beat until combined about 1 minute. Add dry ingredients and beat on low speed until just combined.*

Chill, 15 minutes.

Additional granulated sugar } *Shape dough into 1¼-inch balls and place 2-inches apart on prepared baking sheets. Roll balls in sugar.*

Bake, 8 minutes or until slightly golden.

Immediately top each cookie with a chocolate kiss.

Let cool.

Makes 64 Cookies

TIPS:

Cookies can be made one week ahead and stored in airtight container.

Dough can be made three weeks ahead and frozen. Defrost in refrigerator overnight and bake as above.

This is a classic recipe, but the secret ingredient is the base: saltine crackers!

Toffee Bars

Preheat oven to 400°F.

Line 12½ x 17½ x 1-inch half sheet pan with heavy duty aluminum foil extending over ends of pan.
Spray with non-stick cooking spray. Line bottom with parchment paper
and spray again. (Remember BPB: The butter, paper, butter rule.)
This prevents bars from sticking to bottom of pan and create easy removal for cutting.

35 saltine crackers } *Place crackers in single layer on prepared pan.*

1 cup (2 sticks) butter
1 cup light brown sugar, firmly packed } *Add butter and sugar in saucepan over medium heat. Bring to a boil.*
Heat, 3 to 5 minutes without stirring.
Immediately spread evenly over crackers.
Bake, 5 to 7 minutes, or until bubbly.

1 package (12 ounces) semi-sweet chocolate chips } *Top evenly. Let stand 5 minutes. Spread chocolate with offset spatula to cover.*

1 cup pecans, walnuts or almonds, finely chopped } *Sprinkle with nuts. Cool until firm and break into pieces.*

Makes about 35 Pieces

TIPS:

Can be made one week ahead and stored in airtight container.

Can substitute semi-sweet chocolate with dark chocolate.

Walnut Snowballs

Preheat oven to 350°F.

Line baking sheets with parchment paper.

2 cups all-purpose flour

½ teaspoon baking soda

1 cup walnuts or pecans, chopped

½ teaspoon salt

Combine in medium bowl.

1 cup butter, softened

½ cup confectioners' sugar, sifted

1 teaspoon vanilla extract

In large bowl of electric mixer, beat on high speed until light and creamy, about 3 to 5 minutes.

Slowly add flour mixture on low speed.
Beat until just combined.
Chill, 30 minutes.

Roll into 1-inch balls.
Place 2-inches apart on prepared baking sheets. Chill, 10 to 15 minutes.

Bake 10 minutes or until slightly golden.

additional confectioner's sugar

Roll into additional confectioner's sugar while warm.

Let cool and roll again.
With sifter or fine meshed strainer dust with more confectioner's sugar as desired.

Makes about 4 Dozen

TIPS:

Can be made one week and stored in airtight container for one week or frozen for one month.

Dough can be made three weeks ahead and frozen. Defrost in refrigerator overnight and bake as above.

Inspired by one of my dearest friends, Marianne, these snowballs are the best I have tasted! You can also substitute with any nut you prefer.

Citrus Biscotti

Preheat oven to 350°F.

Line baking sheets with parchment paper.

4 cups unbleached all-purpose flour
2 tablespoons baking powder
2 teaspoons salt

Combine in medium bowl. Set aside.

2 cups (4 sticks) unsalted butter, softened
2 cups sugar

Combine in large bowl of electric mixer. Beat on high speed until light and fluffy, about 5 minutes.

8 large eggs, lightly beaten
1 teaspoon vanilla extract
1 lemon, zested
1 orange, zested

Combine in large glass measuring cup or bowl. Add slowly to butter mixture on low speed (batter will look curdled). Increase to medium speed. Beat for 1 minute.

Slowly add flour mixture to egg mixture on low speed until combined. Beat until smooth, about 2 minutes. DO NOT CHILL!

Fill large pastry bag with batter (no tip, just make 1-inch opening). Squeeze batter onto baking sheets into two parallel lines, about 3-inches apart (batter will spread when baking). If bigger cookies are desired, make wider strips of batter but only make one line in center of baking sheet.

Bake, 8 to 10 minutes or until lightly golden. Let cool a few minutes.

Loosen cookie strips underneath using offset metal spatula. Using sharp serrated knife, slice on diagonal into ½-inch slices. Turn cookies on their side and bake additional 5 to 7 minutes or until a light golden color.

Let cool. Dust with generous amounts of confectioners' sugar.

Makes about 10 Dozen Cookies

TIPS:

This recipe can be easily halved.

Add 1 cup of your favorite nuts, toasted and chopped to batter mixture before baking.

Can substitute citrus zest with 1 tablespoon anise extract.

Can be made and stored in airtight container for two weeks or frozen for two month.

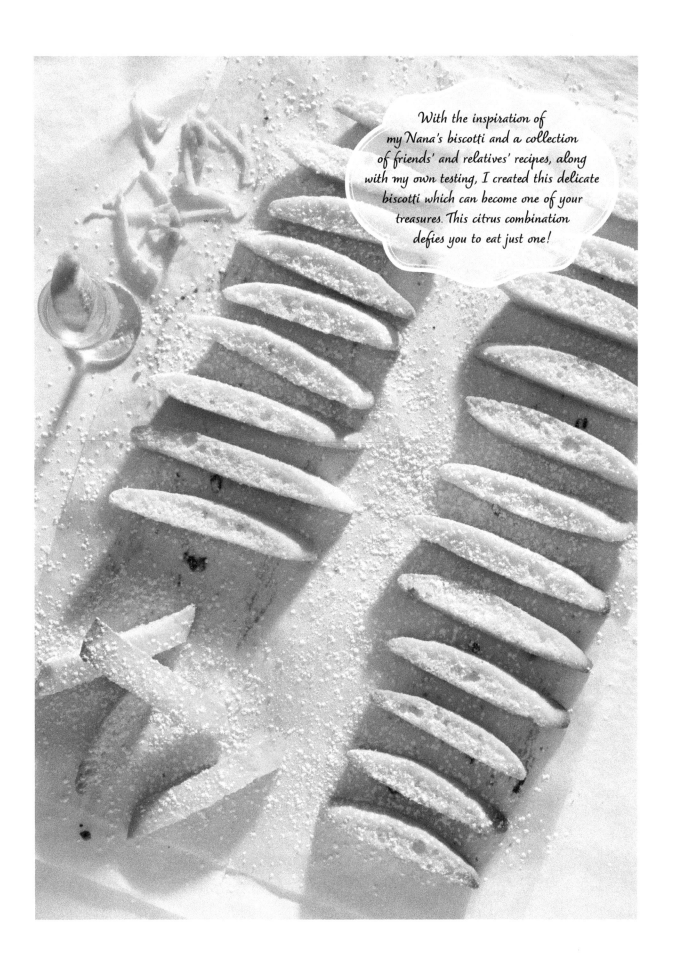

With the inspiration of my Nana's biscotti and a collection of friends' and relatives' recipes, along with my own testing, I created this delicate biscotti which can become one of your treasures. This citrus combination defies you to eat just one!

I have tried to read my Nana's handwriting on her original recipe so the measurements were hard to decipher. But after many trials, I think I have a good version of her famous Almond Crescents. I fondly remember that she used to serve these piled up in a crystal pedestal dish in her living room.

Nana's Almond Crescents

Preheat oven to 325°F.

1²⁄₃ cups all-purpose flour

1 cup blanched almonds, lightly toasted and finely ground (about ¾ cup)

½ teaspoon salt

In medium bowl combine dry ingredients.

1 cup (2 sticks) butter, softened

⅓ cup sugar

In large bowl of electric mixer, beat on high speed until light and fluffy, about 5 minutes.

1 teaspoon vanilla extract

1 teaspoon almond extract

Add to butter mixture on low speed.

Slowly add flour mixture to butter mixture on low speed until just combined. Chill, at least 30 minutes.

Roll dough into 2-inch balls and shape into crescents on parchment-lined baking sheet.

Makes about 4 Dozen

Chill, 15 to 20 minutes.

Bake, 12 to 14 minutes or until slightly golden on the bottom.

1 cup vanilla sugar* or superfine sugar

Add to flat plate and dip warm cookie immediately. Sprinkle, if desired, with colorful sugars.

TIPS:

*Vanilla sugar is available in local supermarkets. To make your own delicious vanilla sugar, place a vanilla bean in 2 cups sugar and allow to sit for two weeks.

Can be made one week ahead and stored in airtight container for one week or frozen for one month.

Dough can be made three weeks ahead and frozen. Defrost in refrigerator overnight and bake as above.

One of my favorite cookies
is the Linzer Bar and hazelnuts
are one of my husband's favorites.
Cut into triangles, it's a beautiful
lattice topped addition to
your cookie tray.

Linzer Bar Triangles

Preheat oven to 350°F.

Line 15½ x 12½ x 1-inch sheet pan with heavy duty aluminum foil extending over ends of pan.
Spray with non-stick cooking spray. Line bottom with parchment paper
and spray again. (Remember BPB: The butter, paper, butter rule.)
This prevents bars from sticking to bottom of pan and create easy removal for cutting.

3 cups all-purpose flour

2 cups hazelnuts or pecans

Add to food processor. Process until finely ground.

1½ cups (3 sticks) butter, softened

1½ cups sugar

Add to large bowl of electric mixer. Beat on high speed until light and creamy, about 5 minutes.

2 eggs

2 teaspoons cinnamon

1 lemon, zested

½ teaspoon ground cloves

¼ teaspoon all spice

1 teaspoon vanilla extract

½ teaspoon salt

Combine in medium bowl and add to butter mixture on low speed until blended. Slowly add flour mixture on low speed until just combined. Press half of dough onto prepared pan. Wrap remaining dough in plastic wrap. Chill, 30 minutes.

Bake, 15 minutes or until slightly golden; let cool.

1 jar (12 ounces) raspberry preserves

Top baked cookie with raspberry preserves. Place chilled dough between two large pieces of parchment paper. Roll to ¼-inch thick. Cut into ½-inch x 12-inch strips. Place diagonally on top of jam. Bake, additional 10 minutes or until lightly golden. Let cool. Remove entire Linzer Bar from pan all at once, by lifting and holding foil edges, for easy cutting.

Makes 48 Triangles

Cut bars with long, hot, sharp knife straight down with one motion for clean, straight edges. Cut into squares then triangles.

Confectioner's sugar

Sprinkle with confectioner's sugar.

TIPS:

For a lattice top and pretty edges, cut dough with ravioli wheel cutter.

Can be stored in airtight container for one week or freeze up to one month.

Pignoli Cookies

Preheat oven to 325°F.

Line baking sheets with parchment paper.

12 ounces almond paste*
½ cup sugar
1 cup confectioners' sugar

} *Combine in food processor. Process until smooth, or sand-like consistency.*

2 egg whites
½ teaspoon almond extract

} *Add to large bowl of electric mixer. Beat on high speed until stiff.*

1½ cups pignoli or pine nuts

} *Fold in almond/sugar mixture.*

Place on flat plate.

Makes about 2 Dozen Cookies

Using 1½-inch ice cream scooper or tablespoon, roll balls into nuts to completely cover. Place 2-inches apart on prepared baking sheets and slightly flatten.

Bake, 15 to 18 minutes or until lightly golden.

Cool on wire racks.

Confectioner's sugar

} *Sprinkle on top of cookies.*

TIPS:

Purchase canned almond paste from your local baker for best results. The fresher the almond paste the softer the cookies.

Can be stored in airtight container for one week or freeze up to one month.

Recipe can easily be doubled (which I highly recommend).

These traditional
Italian cookies are crisp on the outside
and chewy on the inside. They're so
popular, that I also have them in my
Holiday book as well as
Celebrations.

Love Knots *with* Red and Green Nonpareils

Preheat oven to 325°F.
Line baking sheets with parchment paper.

Love Knots:

4 cups unbleached all-purpose flour

1 tablespoon baking powder

1 teaspoon baking soda

1 teaspoon salt

Combine in medium bowl. Set aside.

1 cup (2 sticks) butter, softened

1½ cups sugar

Add to large bowl of electric mixer. Beat on high speed until light and creamy, about 5 minutes.

1 container (15 ounces) whole milk ricotta (about 1¾ cups)

Add and beat on medium high speed, about 2 minutes or until smooth.

2 eggs

2 teaspoons anise or lemon extract*

1 teaspoon vanilla extract

Add and beat on low speed, about 1 minute or until blended.

Slowly add flour mixture on low speed until combined and then beat on high speed, 30 seconds. Use a 1½-inch ice cream scoop or drop heaping tablespoons on prepared baking sheets 2-inches apart. ROLL gently into smooth balls.

Bake, 9 to 11 minutes or until puffed.

Makes about 60 Cookies

DO NOT OVERBAKE Cookie should be light brown on bottom side and light on top. Soft when touched and springs back slightly.

Let cool on wire rack and then coat with icing.

Icing:

¼ cup half and half or light cream

Microwave in heatproof glass measuring cup, 20 seconds.

2 teaspoons anise extract or 1 teaspoon lemon extract mixed with 1 teaspoon fresh lemon juice*

2 to 2¼ cups confectioner's sugar

Slowly add and stir with small wire whisk until blended and thick but still spreadable. Keep covered with plastic wrap while working so icing does not harden.

Assorted sprinkles, colored nonpareils, or any desired color according to your occasion

Spoon icing on cookies one by one and immediately top with sprinkles before icing hardens.

These Italian cookies were traditionally made at weddings because they are a combination of a sweet bread dough tied into a knot. I first learned to make them from my neighbor growing up, the lovely Mrs. Fontana, but they were yeast based. My family simplified them with baking powder, and my in-laws also had a version using baking powder and cream cheese. After many trials and tests, I discovered ricotta makes them a little softer and received my daughters' and friends' best votes! I alter the flavor and sprinkles for the seasons. We traditionally use multi-colored nonpareils, but change the colored sprinkles to red and green at Christmastime.

TIPS:

*I usually use anise flavor for Christmas and lemon flavor for springtime and special occasions.

Use small 1½-inch ice cream scooper to make evenly sized cookies.

It's great to have a partner, one person ice and one person sprinkle!

If icing gets too thick add a few drops of half and half at a time to make thinner.

Cookie dough can be prepare ahead, chilled for up to four hours, and rolled into balls for smoother cookies. Dough can also be frozen up to one month ahead.

These cookies freeze beautifully, unfrosted, up to two months. Best to ice day of serving.

HOW TO USE THIS BOOK

Recipe Book Structure

From my experience styling thousands of recipes, I wanted to create a recipe book that was easier to read. When I have to prepare a multitude of recipes at one time, I rewrite the recipes so I can prepare them quickly and more efficiently. This practice gave me the idea that I am now demonstrating in this book. Here, you see the ingredients needed and the method at the same time. I used brackets to list the ingredients on the left and placed the method directly to the right. In this arrangement, you can anticipate what you need for each step of the recipe easily, know exactly what measurements you need, and therefore avoid mistakes. It also helps me with my grocery and preparation lists.

Ingredients and Terms Used

Extra Virgin Olive Oil: This is a family favorite and the most essential ingredient in my kitchen. It has always been a staple since I was a child. It's one of the healthiest oils to cook with but should not be used with high heat, as this will alter its structure and flavor. Use butter, canola or peanut oil for high heat instead.

Flour: Use unbleached all-purpose

Eggs: Use large

Butter: Always use unsalted, especially in baking

Salt and pepper: I list them often in recipes. Seasoning is important in making all of your cooking hard effort come together. Use amounts to your liking. I usually season at the end of cooking unless specified when used in a coating or baking.

Sauté: In cooking school, I learned the saying, "hot pan, cold oil." This means always heat your pan first and then add your oil, butter, etc., to the pan before cooking. This helps prevent your meat or food items from sticking, and also makes a beautiful seared or browned edge on your meat items to seal in the juices. Heat your pan a few minutes on medium high heat, then add your oil for about one more minute. Then, begin cooking to your liking or according to the recipe.

BPB: A baking term I learned in pastry class in culinary school. For all of your cake pans, baking pans, etc., spray your pan with non-stick cooking spray or rub with butter, line with baking parchment paper, then spray or butter again. (Thus the term BPB.) Your baked items will never stick again. It's a foolproof way to remove them without the disaster of ruining your hard work.

Red or White Wine Vinegar, Red or White Balsamic Vinegar: I use these quite often because they have a fresh look and still give your salad a nice, rich balanced flavor. Of course, substitute with any of your favorite wine-based vinegars.

Flavored Vinegars and Oils: Experiment by substituting any flavor you desire to make a whole new flavoring for a dressing and/or dish. I personally use fig, raspberry, sherry and herb infused vinegars often.

Citrus Zest: I love citrus flavors in salads and incorporate lemons, limes and oranges by using the zest of the skin and the juice.

Parmesan Cheese: I recommend using only Parmigiano Reggiano. It's so buttery and nutty, and will make so many dishes sing.

Romano Cheese: This cheese is a little saltier than Parmesan and gives a nice bite and creaminess to many of my recipes. I actually often use Parmesan and Romano together to give some of my Italian-based recipes a perfect blend of tanginess, saltiness and nuttiness.

My Favorite Tools

Good Set of Professional Knives: I cannot stress enough how important it is to have a set of good professional knives. A good set of sharp knives enables you to work more efficiently in the kitchen and is much safer than an inexpensive set. You can buy one knife at a time and start to build a personal set for your needs. I would suggest a good quality chef knife to start, utility knife for multitasking jobs, a paring knife for small items, and a long serrated knife for bread and cake slicing.

Zester/Narrow Zester with Handle: It's long and usually has a handle. It's perfect for zesting citrus in a flash and can also be used for grating garlic, chocolate or hard cheeses, too.

Metal Scraper: I keep this tool on my cutting board during all my prep. It has a thin metal base, about six inches long and four inches wide, with a wooden handle on one end. It's terrific when scraping flour off your board after baking and makes clean up a breeze. Also, it's handy when scooping up any chopped small veggies or herbs to go right into the skillet during cooking.

Offset Spatula: A must in your kitchen so maybe buy a few. It's a small metal spatula that bends by the handle. Makes easy spreading and frosting on cakes and desserts.

Immersion Blender: This no hassle device saves time and cleanup. It's great when blending canned tomatoes for sauces and sautéed veggies for making soup right in the pan or pot you're cooking in.

Small and Large Food Processor: I use my small food processor often, especially when I need to chop a good amount of garlic, onion, parsley or herbs for entertaining. It's also great for making quick, fresh bread crumbs. A large food processor makes cookie crumbs as well as pastry and pizza doughs in a flash.

Large Standing Mixer: Just a joy for mixing, baking, whipping, etc. It practically mixes by itself. You can run your mixer hands-free while preparing your next steps.

Large Piping Star Tips: These make a simple dessert into a showpiece. Pipe your whipped cream in pretty rosettes simply and easily.

Disposable Pint or Quart Size Plastic Storage Bags: Use these to drizzle chocolate, squeeze mayonnaise or mustard easily, or even pipe whipped cream. Fill with desired ingredient, snip one end and have an instant piping bag.

Kitchen Shears: So helpful when cutting all types of food items without ruining your good knives. I especially love them when cutting pizza, through chicken bones, and snipping herbs.

Aluminum Foil and Parchment Paper: I line my baking sheets often with aluminum foil when I am cooking for a party. This does not affect the cooking process. Makes clean up easy peasy! It's imperative to line your cake pans and baking sheets with parchment paper for non-stick success in baking.

Entertaining Tips and Party Hints

Home sweet home

Entertaining at home is a very warm and loving way to enjoy family and friends. There is just something about the warmth of your home that makes people feel very comfortable and relaxed. Whether it be just a neighbor stopping by last minute and a glass of wine turns into an impromptu plate of pasta or planning for a big family celebration, having a gathering at home makes your guests feel special.

Inspiration with zeal

I usually get most of my ideas while food shopping. Walking down the supermarket aisles or stopping by a local farmers' market inspires me with so many ideas for cooking. Always take advantage of the season and use fruits and vegetables that are at their highest peak and availability at that time locally whenever possible. You will get the best bang for your buck while buying locally and funding the local farmers, as well as feed your family with the most nutritious and organic foods available. Take advantage of food magazines and social media, and start collecting ideas of cooking and baking that you enjoy. Food likes and dislikes are very subjective and you have to be excited and love what you are making so the dish will truly shine. Much of my inspiration has come from my family and food colleagues. Talk about what you made for dinner at your work place, school or with friends. They will share what they made and you may get a new idea to try. Especially around the holidays, everyone is talking about their favorite cookie or entrée that their family loves. Many ingredients are interchangeable in my savory recipes. Baking, though, is more of a science and you must be careful not to deviate from the measurements. Get inspired everyday and create something in your own way!

Plan and anticipate. It's all in the prep!

Because I am a food stylist, most of the success of a food shoot is in the planning, prep, research and anticipation. I have learned, with years of experience, that if you're totally prepared, the shoot can be flawless and goes smoothly. Actually, sometimes it goes too smoothly, and the clients think it was an easy day, but what they did not see was all the behind the scenes prep and hard work that made that one slice of perfect pie look gorgeous. It's the same way with entertaining. If you're prepared ahead of time and anticipate the organization needed, your party will go smoothly. Also, if there is a blip or two, maybe you forgot the sour cream for the quesadillas or burnt the bruschetta toast—just skip it and no one will even notice. Just don't worry! Once the party gets started I start to relax because most of the work is all done. So, for most of the recipes I have noted which are wonderful make-aheads and include helpful prep tips.

Mise en place!

A vital french culinary term I learned in culinary school that means "Everything in its place." It's so important to get all your ingredients organized and ready to go, including pan and baking sheet prep, before you start cooking and baking. This way you cook faster and make less mistakes.

Lists, lists, lists!

Another great planning tip is to make a series of lists. I'm an avid list maker and if you ask my husband he will tell you that I'm obsessed with sticky notes! I love the bright colored ones and use them for all my daily errands and activities that need to get done. I like the old fashioned way of writing them down as this helps me remember better, especially if it's before bedtime. Yes, I keep sticky notes on my bedside table as well as on my pocketbook and in my car. You do not want to forget an important item. If you forget an important ingredient at a food shoot it can make or break a photography job.

New Year's Day Dinner
1st Course

Christmas Dinner 1986
Homemade Eggnog
Champagne Moet & Chandon
Escarole Soup with Meatballs à la Mom
Polenta with Wild Mushrooms
Caesar Salad
with Arugala & Pignoli
with Lemon and Parsley
onion, Leek and Scallion

Dessert
Webbed Cookie Pizza
Chocolate Chip C
Rice Crispy
Dipp

Appetizers
Salmon with A Crème Fraîche Sauce of Dill and
Christmas Tree Caviar Spread
Assorted Pates
Selected Antipasto Meats by Eva
Vegetable antipasta, Tri-color Peppers, Sauteed
Sauteed Escarole with Garlic, Roasted Eggplant,
Olives with Provolone, Assorted Cheeses, Marinated Ch

New Year's Eve Millenium Dinner
1999

Appetizers
Beluga Caviar Service with Iced Vodka with Roses
Lemon Zested Scallops with Sugared Maple Bacon Twists
Broiled Polenta Triangles with Sauteed Spinach Pignoli and Herb Feta
Parma Prosciutto Wraps with Pesto and Roasted Peppers
Nova Scotia Salmon Wraps with Boursin Cheese and Chives
Dip with Buttered Bread Crumbs
with Apricots and Horseradish
Seafood Course
Tails with Zested Lemon B
Pasta Course
agna with Wild Mushroo
Main Course
Fillet Mignon with To
aramelized Red On
Broiled Tomato
European Co
Salad with Sp
zola with
es with
Dess
ke wi

"Christmas Eve 1994"
1st Course
Iced Shrimp Cocktail with Herbs
with Cocktail Sauce & Green Dill Watercress Sauce
2nd Course
Zuppa de Broccoli with Garlic Roasted
3rd Course
Linguine with Fresh Tomato & Vianoli Baby Clams
Capillini with Breaded Calamari Baked with achovy-lemon
butter Sauce
4th Course
Lightly Battered Flounder Fillet with Lemon
Shrimp Scampi   Broiled Lobster Tail with
Herbed Butter
Stuffed Clams with Semolina Pesto
Marinated Anchovy Salad with Mushrooms, Cauliflower, Peppers
Olives
Grandma's Rakala Salad
Dessert
Apple-Pear Bundt Cake
Tiramisu   Double Cookie Icecream Mocha Cake
Assorted Christmas Cookies
Espresso/ Cappuccino   Assorted N

Christmas Dinner 2007
Appetizers
Caviar Torte   Shrimp Cocktail with Watercress Dipping Sauce
Cousin Debbie's Cheese Ball
First Course
Assorted Antipasto- Cured Meats & Cheeses, Grilled and Marinated Vegetables,
Roasted Eggplant, Stuffed Olives, Fresh Mozzarella, Tomato & Basil, Prosciutto
Wrapped Sweet Melon
Pasta Course
Lasagna Bolognese
Entrée
Roasted Beef Tenderloin Smothered with fine herbs Pommery Mustard and Bacon
Port Wine Sauce Reduction
Jackie's Mashed Potatoes with Gruyère
Wild Mushroom Saute
Creamed Fresh Baby Spinach Gratin
Broiled Asparagus and Radicchio with Almonds and Pancetta
Stuffed Artichokes with Semolina Bread Crumbs
Desserts
Wendi's Bread White Chocolate Bread Pudding
Creamy Rice Pudding   Raspberry Crème Brulee
Peppermint Mocha Candy Cane Trifle
Assorted Christmas Cookies   Struffoli add Bows
Fresh Fruit   Homemade Candies

Cream Sau
Main Course
sted
Main Course
Appetizers
Spreads(O
Hot Artich
Brie Almon
ni Stromboni
Hot Apple Cid
Main Course
Fixins and
ed in Hot Apple
Apple

Dessert
Wolf

Thanksgiving
1st Cour
Antipasto by Uncle Steve
CAPONATA/ MARINATED Zucchini
olive
ATE
2nd Course
Grandma's Escade Soup
Main Course
Herb Roasted Turkey with
Yams   Creamed Mashed Pota
Green Beans au Gratin

HALLOWEEN 2004!!!!!
APPETIZERS
ASSORTED DIPS AND TREATS
SPICY CHICKEN WINGS!
GOOLISH CHEESE BALLS
POLENTA WITH GOAT CHEESE
PEPPER SAUCE
DINNER
TEXAS-STYLE CHILI WI
DOGS IN SPICED
RICE
FILET WI

Thanksgiving Dinner
November 22, 2000
First Course
Antipasto Selections- Sauteed Broccoli Rabe with Sundried Tomatoes,
Fresh Spinach with Gorgonzola and Pignoli Nuts, Marinated Chic Pea
Salad with Fresh Oregano, Roasted Tri-Color Peppers in Olive Oil and
Basil, Assorted European Olives, Basket Cheese Wrapped with Prosciutto
De Parma, Fresh Mozzarella with Tomato and Arugula, Suppressatta
Pepperoni, Provolone Tray, Stuffed Hot Peppers.
Second Course
Escarole Soup with Mini-Meatballs and Chicken
With Semolina Battered Dipped Crouton
Main Course
Herb Roasted Turkey with Wild Mushroom Gravy and Sausa
Cranberry Stuffing
Whipped Mashed Potatoes
Hazelnut S

Cake
Corn C
Brownies
Treats
kes
Apples
!!)

How to Party Prep Ahead
Here is a list breakdown I use for holiday gatherings:

1 month ahead

Plan your menu!

Order invitations (if sending them)

Plan guest list to determine number of guests

Send out emails for save the date

Know your theme and plan accordingly

Rent any equipment you may need (i.e.: DJ, tent, tables, chairs, plates, glasses and hire any extra help you may need for bartending and clean up)

Start to purchase staple items (i.e.: jars or cans)

3 weeks ahead

Finalize your menu

Send out invitations or evites

Plan what make-aheads you will do and what can be frozen

Plan and purchase beverages, chill wine and any other refrigerated beverages

Make your shopping list

Start to purchase staple items and paper goods

Make or get name place cards ready

2 weeks ahead

Start to prepare anything that can be frozen (i.e.: cookies, cake layers, sauces and components of recipes such as pesto, etc.)

Order any specialty meats or flower arrangements

1 week ahead

Start to organize house and get rid of clutter

Clean all glassware, dishes and silverware you may be using

Iron tablecloths and set table

Type and print our your final menu and make adjustments later

Take out your platters, baskets and serving utensils. Start to label each piece with a sticky note with the food item on it. This will help you decide ahead of time how many platters, bowls and accessories you need. It's so helpful to your kitchen helpers so they know which food item goes on what with no confusion.

Clean out a front door closet for coats if rainy or cold

1 or 2 days ahead

Finish most of your perishable shopping

Finish your house and get everything in order. This is when I start to hide things and find them 3 months later!

Get your centerpieces and candles organized

Pick your playlist for great music

Check your set table and place name cards

Go over your checklist and cross off all that is done and ready

Defrost all items that were make-ahead in refrigerator

1 day ahead

Make sure your table is set and, if you have a buffet, that all your plates, napkins, utensils, etc. are all set

Finish centerpieces

Place a small flower vase and candle in bathrooms. It's welcoming and looks special. Stock with extra toilet paper, scented hand soap, decorative paper towels and hand creams that coordinate with the seasons.

Make sure dishwasher is empty

Get bar ready with wine glasses, wine opener and fruit garnishes (i.e.: lemons, limes, oranges, etc.)

Also, slice fruit for flavored water. Sliced cucumbers or lemons are favorites in our house and look pretty in glass pitchers. Try sliced citrus of any kind and/or sliced strawberries to make a lovely pink colored water for your party.

Buy ice if needed

Make sure all appropriate wine, beer, champagne and/or soda are all chilled if possible

Finish last minute perishable food shopping

Chop, blanch and mix anything that can last in the refrigerator before event and prep everything you possibly can

Wrap any baking or roasting pans for easy clean up in aluminum foil

Cut any finger desserts and have ready on tray in refrigerator

Day of party

Put ice in coolers and wine buckets. Chill all beverages.

Assemble platters and make any last minute items. Always wrap in plastic wrap and refrigerate until serving time.

Buy fresh bread if needed in the morning

Check menu to make sure you have everything

Frame the menu for display. This adds a nice touch to the table. Start saving your menus to cherish that moment in time around your table.

Have fun and enjoy your guests

Less is more

One of my dearest friends and talented photographers who photographed this book, Al Owens, taught me "Less is more." He said to keep food photography simple and not overdue it. I have used that concept in my entertaining and cooking as well. Try not to overthink your party and make it too complicated. I have always been a perfectionist but I found that people remember the food, fun, laughter and great time they have with family and friends—not if I garnished every one of my bruschetta toasts. Simplify and make a few ingredients sing in your dishes. It's not the quantity but the quality of each recipe's ingredients. Just a simple farm picked tomato with fresh mozzarella, a basil leaf and a drizzle of extra virgin olive oil will make your guests' mouthes water without lighting up your stove or oven. Keep it simple and easy while making everyone comfortable.

Ambience

Always create a warm atmosphere. Just lighting a candle, unscented if serving food, or a food-scented candle that goes with your menu, gives your guests a warm welcome as soon as they walk through the door. I also use simple flowers and prefer fruit, herbs and vegetables as my centerpieces by placing them in large glass vases with water in all different sizes. Just a simple vase filled with your favorite flower can turn a room into a special occasion. If I have surprise or last minute guests, sometimes I fill any glass container with whole or cut up fruit, a sprig of herbs or greenery I have outside, and I have a centerpiece. Also, don't forget your bathrooms. Add a small bud vase and a lighted votive candle for added charm.

We are from a musical family and have piano players, singers, dancers and musical theatre trained children. Our house would not be complete without great music. Pick your party playlist ahead of time and have it on when guests walk in. This gives the whole party a fun and relaxed atmosphere. The music can even pick up in tempo as the evening progresses.

People eat with their eyes

My food styling training and artful eye has made me love not only cooking, but also the art of food as well. When you serve and plate, just think about the texture, color and height of your placement. A spot of color goes a long way. For example, by adding a half of a cherry tomato on your dip with a sprig of parsley, your dip will go from ordinary to dazzling. Try and garnish with color and something that represents what is in the recipe. For example, if there is basil and lemon in the dip or salad, garnish with a bunch of basil leaves and slices of lemon. It will look beautiful and impress your guests.

Garnish suggestions

Savory items

> Lemons, limes and oranges: Sliced in wedges, slices, halves and/or zested with or without the leaves
> Herbs: Leaves of all kinds; rosemary sprigs, basil leaves, mint leaves, thyme, marjoram, oregano, lavender and chives with its blossoms are gorgeous.
> Fruit: Strawberries, raspberries, blueberries, grapes of all kinds and their leaves make beautiful lining for cheese platters.
> Olives of all kinds, pickles, roasted red peppers of all colors
> Chopped herbs and nuts
> Fruit leaves of all kinds (i.e.: lemons, oranges, grapes and figs)

Sweet items

> Chocolate shavings, chocolate curls
> Confectioner's sugar
> Cocoa powder
> Whipped cream
> Crystallized dried fruit

Place settings and cards

Mix old with new china, utensils, glassware and flatware
Make a place card for everyone
Preferred when everyone sits together, if they can, except for outdoor parties and buffets

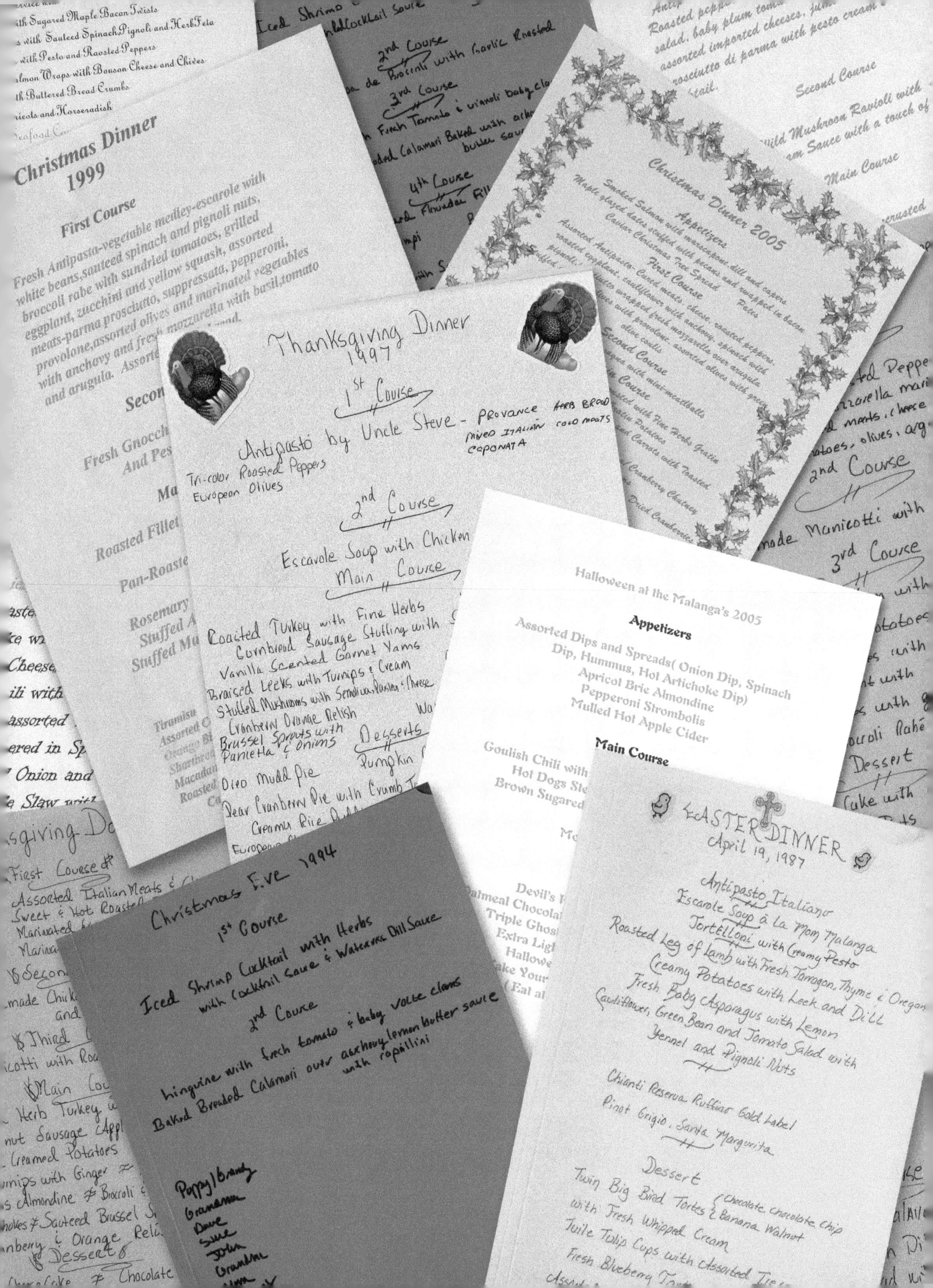

Christmas Dinner 1999

First Course

Fresh Antipasta-vegetable medley-escarole with white beans, sauteed spinach and pignoli nuts, broccoli rabe with sundried tomatoes, grilled eggplant, zucchini and yellow squash, assorted meats-parma prosciutto, suppressata, pepperoni, provolone, assorted olives and marinated vegetables with anchovy and fresh mozzarella with basil, tomato and arugula. Assorted ...

Second ...

Fresh Gnocch...
And Pes...

Mai...

Roasted Fillet ...

Pan-Roaste...

Rosemary ...
Stuffed A...
Stuffed Mu...

Tiramisu ...
Assorted C...
Orange B...
Shortbread...
Macadan...
Roasted ...
Ca...

(Partial menu, top left)

...ith Sugared Maple Bacon Twists
...s with Sauteed Spinach Pignoli and Herb Feta
...with Pesto and Roasted Peppers
...lmon Wraps with Boursan Cheese and Chives
...th Buttered Bread Crumbs
...eats and Horseradish
...eafood Co...

(Partial menu, top center)

Iced Shrimp ... Cocktail Sauce

2nd Course
... de Broccoli with Garlic Roasted

3rd Course
... Fresh Tomato & vianoli baby cla...
...ded Calamari Baked with arti...
butter sauce

4th Course
...ed Flounder Fil...

...pi

...S...

Christmas Dinner 2005

(Partial, top right)

Appetizers

Smoked Salmon with mascarpone dill and capers
Maple glazed dates stuffed with pecans and wrapped in bacon
Caviar Christmas Tree Spread
Assorted Antipasto- Cured meats, cheese, roasted peppers,
roasted eggplant, cauliflower with anchovy, sundried peppers,
pignoli...
...to wrapped fresh mozzarella over arugula
...ows with provolone, assorted olives with gar...
olive oils

First Course
Petto...

Second Course
...gna with mini-meatballs

... Course
...ed with Fine Herbs Garlic
...tatoe Potatoes Gratin
...nd Carrots with Toasted

... Cranberry Chutney

... Dried Cranberries

(Partial, top right edge)

Antip...
Roasted peppers...
salad, baby plum tom...
assorted imported cheeses, jum...
...rosciutto di parma with pesto crea...
...tail.

Second Course
...ild Mushroom Ravioli with
...m Sauce with a touch of

Main Course

(Partial, right edge)

...ed Pepper...
...zzarella mari...
... meats, cheese
...tatoes, olives, arg...

2nd Course

...made Manicotti with

3rd Course

...with

...otatoes
...s with
...with g...
... souroli Rabe

Dessert

...ake with

...ts

Thanksgiving Dinner 1997

1st Course

Antipasto by Uncle Steve - Provance   Herb Bread
                                       mixed Italian   cold meats
Tri-color Roasted Peppers   Caponata
European Olives

2nd Course

Escarole Soup with Chicken

Main Course

Roasted Turkey with Fine Herbs
Cornbread Sausage Stuffing with S...
Vanilla Scented Garnet Yams
Braised Leeks with Turnips & Cream
Stuffed Mushrooms with Semolian, Parsley & cheese
Cranberry Orange Relish   Wa...
Brussel Sprouts with
Pancetta & Onions   ### Desserts

Oreo Mudd Pie   Pumpkin ...
Pear Cranberry Pie with Crumb T...
Creamy Rice Pudd...
European ...

Halloween at the Malanga's 2005

Appetizers

Assorted Dips and Spreads(Onion Dip, Spinach
Dip, Hummus, Hot Artichoke Dip)
Apricot Brie Almondine
Pepperoni Strombolis
Mulled Hot Apple Cider

Main Course

Goulish Chili with ...
Hot Dogs Ste...
Brown Sugared ...

Mo...

Devil's ...
...atmeal Chocolat...
Triple Ghost...
Extra Light...
Hallowe...
...ake Your...
(Eat al...

Thanksgiving D...

First Course ...

Assorted Italian Meats & C...
Sweet & Hot Roasted ...
Marinated ...
Marina...

Second ...

...made Chick...
and ...

Third ...

...icotti with Roa...

Main Cou...

... Herb Turkey u...
...nut Sausage Appl...
...Creamed Potatoes
...rnips with Ginger ...
...s Almondine & Broccoli ...
...holes & Sauteed Brussel S...
...ranberry & Orange Reli...

Dessert...

...cake & Chocolate...

Christmas Eve 1994

1st Course

Iced Shrimp Cocktail with Herbs
with Cocktail Sauce

2nd Course

Linguine with fresh tomato & baby volte clams
Baked Breaded Calamari over anchovy lemon butter sauce
with rapallini

Poppy/Brandy
Grandma...
Dave
Sue
John
Grandma...
...

EASTER DINNER
April 19, 1987

Antipasto Italiano
Escarole Soup à la Mom Malanga
Tortelloni with Creamy Pesto
Roasted Leg of Lamb with Fresh Tarragon, Thyme & Oregano
Creamy Potatoes with Leek and Dill
Fresh Baby Asparagus with Lemon
Cauliflower, Green Bean and Tomato Salad with
Fennel and Pignoli Nuts

Chianti Reserva Ruffino Gold Label
Pinot Grigio, Santa Margarita

Dessert

Twin Big Bird Tortes & Chocolate chocolate chip
with Fresh Whipped Cream   & Banana Walnut
Twile Tulip Cups with assorted Tie...
Fresh Blueberry Tart...
Ass...

In Appreciation

Thank you to my family whom I love beyond measure with all my heart, especially my husband Tom, and daughters, Maria and Marisa, for always believing in me. Thank you Tommy, my husband and best friend. Thank you for endlessly running around for specific, perfect ingredients (that may or may not have made you go crazy) and last minute shopping for every party, special occasion, shoot and this cookbook. Your patience, selfless love, laughter and kind heart gave me the calmness and strength to finish. I love you always and couldn't have done this without you.

My girls, Maria and Marisa, made me a bet to start my cookbook eight years ago and it came true! With their faith and endless support I had the confidence I needed to begin this book. I would never have had the courage to finish. Maria typed all the original recipes and Marisa proofread each one at the end, including all my copy, a multitude of times. My girls were my greatest inspiration and helped develop and test the recipes. They were my original taste tasters since they were babies. Their encouragement supercharged me with aspirations to follow my dream. They are my most precious blessings. I am so proud of them as they continue to shine in their own passions through all they do. Always believe, follow and listen to your heart with trust and ease. This is the path to true happiness. Share with the world your talents. Never, ever quit following your own dreams, my sweethearts. With faith and envisioning success all things are possible. I love you pumpkins with all my heart, always.

For my angels, Mom and Dad, who always believed in me and supported my passion. My Mom was my first assistant who tirelessly and lovingly helped me start my food career. We always had all the holidays and entertained constantly. My Mom taught me to get a party ready in no time with a moment's notice, and I loved doing it. That passion follows me to this day. My Dad guided me in all my career choices. My mentor, my advisor, my best friend, whom I try to emulate professionalism, a hard work ethic and determination from in all I do! He emphasized to do what you love and you will be great at it. His motto was to never quit and if you focus on what you believe in with faith, hard work and determination, anything is possible. They both encouraged me in every adventure I threw myself into and continue to encourage me in spirit in all I do. I love you both from here to heaven with all my heart.

For Michele Jerry and Al Owens, who inspired me with their incredible talents and unlimited creativity to make this book beautiful! I have been truly blessed with your friendships. Thank you, for your sincere support and many long but fun-filled days of photography at my house. It never feels like work when we are together. You were my informal taste testers for every recipe. Michele, your artful eye and gorgeous props made every recipe come to life. Your treasured friendship gave me the confidence to continue my goal. Dreams do come true! I could not have done this without you my precious friend. My Al, you are an incredible man and human being, and I will always look up to you on a pedestal as my adviser, mentor and cherished friend. Your wisdom and advice made this incredible journey a success. These gorgeous photographs brought my treasured food memories to life just the way I envisioned them. Your talent and creativity goes beyond the camera! My gratitude and love can not be measured! With laughter and tears you both were there for me every step of the way. Love you both beyond!

For Nancy Hourihan, how we were so blessed to meet by chance through my dear friend Christie Pagano. Thank you, Christie, for this wonderful gift. Nancy, thank you for my gorgeous cookbook design, artistic perfection on and off set and endless hours of putting the pieces together. Thank you beyond measure for your patience, talent and artistic magic. This is my showpiece. Love you dearly!

For Lisa Curran, who helped me with her artful eye and loving patience. I am so deeply grateful, love you!

For Devon Knight and Dave Katz for making me shine in my cookbook video. Your talents are beyond magical! Love you!

For Geovanna Colindres, who assisted in my kitchen for most of the book. Thank you for always knowing my next move in the kitchen and on set.

For Donna Saiewitz, who assisted in my kitchen and also tirelessly edited the first version of every one of my recipes with patience and precision. She also researched and created my index. Thank you Jack Hourihan for all of your help with the edits.

For Tracy McKenna, who came on board willingly to assist at the end of our shooting. You are magical and I'm so blessed you are in my life.

For my big sister Celeste, my confidante, who never stopped believing in me. She is the best cleaner-upper in the kitchen you will ever see. She is always here for me in any situation no matter how far away. I am forever grateful for all her endless trips to be by my side whenever I needed her. She is not only an amazing sister, but also my best friend. For her support and encouragement every step of the way, and for always making me feel so special in all I do. Love you, Big Sis.

For my Nana Daisy Pellicciotto, who taught me my first experiences in the kitchen growing up as a child. She was 90 going on 30! I hope to carry her youthful spirit always. The love and cooking traditions of my Italian family have inspired me my entire life. For my grandmother Maria Alia, who died at age 39 and I never met. I found out from my Dad that she contributed recipes to a food column in the *Guttenberg Gazette* during the late 1920's and early 1930's. I sense her being by my side as she inspires me, in spirit, with her love of food and tradition.

For my mother-in-law Elisa Malanga, who was an amazing cook. She shared her recipes lovingly and was always a terrific help to me in the kitchen for the holidays. She helped me tirelessly with my children, especially while I had to be on set day in and day out on particularly demanding jobs. She was a second Mom to me and I am eternally grateful for her love and support. I love you and miss you dearly. Her outstanding pizza will live on forever in our family. I did not know my father-in-law long, but he loved what I did for a living and always asked me a million questions about my shoots and recipes with a smile and a contagious, joyful Malanga laugh. His favorite was lemon meringue pie and I perfected my technique because of him. Love you with misses, Dad.

For my son-in-law Christopher McMahon. Thank you for eating everything that I make for you, even the whole leaves on the artichokes. It's a joy to feed you and I can't wait to cook numerous new memories together at our family table!

For Arthur Imperatore, Sr., Dad's best childhood friend and my inspiration in so many ways. We've enjoyed numerous talks for hours around my table while enjoying Sunday Gravy! Your keen sense of past history, propelling knowledge of our future, and insight have always resulted in positive advice for myself and my children that will last lifetimes. Thank you, Arthur, for being part of our family.

For my Cornell professors Marcia Pimentel, Dr. Gertrude Armbruster and Dr. Virginia Utermohlen. Your encouragement in my field through my studies and advice were invaluable. Thank you for inspiring my potential, keeping in touch and supporting my goals from the beginning. Cornell University will always be an important, vital and treasured part of my life.

For the amazing teachers and chefs at the New York Restaurant School and Le Cordon Bleu. Thank you for the intense culinary training that helped make me become the professional I am today.

For my food editor employers who gave me my first chance as a freelancer, William Rice at *Food & Wine*, Elizabeth Alston at *Woman's Day* and Jeanne Voltz at *Red Book*. I am deeply thankful for all I learned with you at the starting gate of my career path.

For Silvia Lehrer, for giving me my first job as your assistant at your cooking school, Cooktique, at age 16. This catapulted my culinary journey.

For my special colleagues Anna Marie Cesario, Marianne Arimenta and Vicky Hayes, who I met in the beginning of my career and became my closest, dearest friends. They have inspired, shared and taught me so much in their test kitchens, studios and homes. For their love of food and entertaining. Our conversations and world are always based on food. I will always cherish sharing ideas and recipes together, and our everlasting love and friendship. I love you all dearly!

For Deborah Ruggieri, Iggy Ruggieri and Sheila Wenke. You were an integral part of perfecting my career as a food stylist, on and off set. Our years on set helped me hone my skills, making me as proficient in the kitchen as I am in the studio. We learned so much together. Every job taught me something new while we discovered, created and had fun together all at the same time. Our careers brought us together but, most importantly, gave me lifelong, true friendships that I will treasure forever. Love you!

For Christina Nuzzo who took my portraits for this book. It was so truly me that I used it for this book. You are so talented.

For Justine Bylo for her professional and kind advise regarding self publishing.

For Ryan Brondolo, one of my son-in-law's dearest friends, who designed my Alysciouss logo. What a great gift that I love!

For my past and present assistants throughout my career. You all went beyond measure in making my job seamless while working so hard and always with a smile: Carmel Alia, Celeste Lafferty, Wendy Walters, Linda Cesario, Elisa Scarpino, Linda-Gail Alati, Fildelma Winters, Judy Gencarelli, Pattie Corrado, Helen Gabrysiak, Mary Jo Romano, Jackie Mercogliano, Sharon Carr, Geovanna Colindres, Vicky Hayes, Joanne Panayi, Linda Rivera, Donna Saiewitz, Russell Maitland, Tracy McKenna, Maria Malanga, Marisa Malanga, Christopher McMahon and Miriana Marqeuz.

For all my treasured food families, friends, chefs, photographers, art directors, assistants, agencies and graphic designers who have inspired me throughout my career in my craft of food styling, photography, cooking and art. Our experiences together shine through my work. Thank you for molding me into who I am today on and off the studio sets, kitchens, culinary schools and your homes. There are so many more people to thank I can't count but I wanted to especially thank the following people for all their kindness, sharing, teaching, opportunities, friendships and just for their love of food: Alia, Malanga, Lafferty, Pellicciotto, McMahon, Mercogliano & Merk families, Silvia Lehrer, Jacques Pepin, Giugliano Bugialli, Bruce Beck, Mrs. Betty Ann Maryott, Mrs. Kovak, Connie Fontana, Nancy Lenore, Peter Pioppo, Jerry Simpson, Gene Knowles, Dave Lewis, Donna Aristo, Tom Dilworth, Ysabel Martinez, Danisha Devor-Mackesey, Carol Ring, Terri Davis, Sharon Miller, Rick Becker, Ken Kephart, Lisa Curran, John Millington, Bill Truran, Dan Pitzczatoski ,Lou Manna, Andie Fazio, Nicole Kantanas, Carolyn Taylor, Jerry Errico, John Montana, Billy Arce, Pattie and Charles Corrado and family, Josephine DeAngelis, Dr. Linda Cesario, Joe Mazzo, Debbie Cesario, Daniel Cesario Jr., Linda Rivera and family, Marni Leslie, Lisa Kenny, Joanne Panayi, Diane Revels, Ceil Maher, Jackie Mercogliano, Sharon Carr, Tom, Sean, Nick and Chris Lafferty & family, Steve Adubato, Jr., Maria and Jack Panico, Diane Holtaway, Heather Bean, Lilia Temple, Mary Jo Romano, Les Herzog, Michele Harris, April Forman, Lisa DeStephano, Sean O'Brien, Sandy Cobin, Charlie Biondo, Joyce Lipinski Cascella, Janet Ellison Pearsall, Naomi Kettler, Jill Flack, Martha Garcia, Sheryl Abbot, James Smith, Jenna Smith, Faye Egan, Cathy Marschean-Spivak, Denise Casimono, Sarah Page, Dr. Mei Ling Imperatore, Dr. Rosalie Gagliardi, Maggie Smith, Diane Revels, Lauren Dellabella, Lisa Christiansen, Debbie, Ray, Renee & Janessa Celentano,Ruggieri family, Monaco Family, Scarpino Family, Cesario Family, Pagano Family, Alati Family, Donna Riccardi, Paul Gelsobello, Russell Maitland, Joe Wohlgemuth, Norma Jean Longfield, Carol Linger, Karen Deluca, Elizabeth Pelaez, Alan Stabile, Ybich Malanga, Justine Chapin, Lori Egan, Patty Mitchell, Julie Pham, Michelle Squillante, Susie Collier and My Gang (Doug Tanner, Bob Levai, Brain O'Connor, Dylan Craig, Artie Ley, George Mouakad, Nitza Goodman, Ernie Kolhsaat and Donna Galligan).

Just for the love it,

Alyssa xo

CPSIA information can be obtained
at www.ICGtesting.com
Printed in the USA
BVHW020855211122
652194BV00035B/608